AGLOW WITH LIGHT

Inspirational insights into our Deepest Being

Carmel Comerford

CONTENTS

DEDICATION

I dedicate this book to the memory of my mother and father and all those who have walked with me on my journey. They, by their immense faith, have given me a treasure untold.

ACKNOWLEDGEMENTS

I wish to acknowledge Fr. David Melly (Liverpool) who has been a great support to me at a spiritual level in writing this book.

Sybil Pearce who helped inspire the choice of cover photograph.

Sr. Catherine Lafferty C.P. for reviewing the text.

Lastly, but so important, David Thomas, without whose skilful expertise this book would not have come to print.

Above all, thanks to my God who directed these reflections in prayer to me for His people. May His peace penetrate the hearts of all who reflect on them.

Carmel Comerford
January 2017

INTRODUCTION

These stories/ parables reflect my own inner search, and often struggle, to find my response to a loving call. They reflect many everyday experiences, through which He chose to reveal himself and myself to me. Through them He awakened in me a new sense and realization of his presence in his people and the whole of creation. They are so often the broken people, the marginalized and, in the eyes of society, the not too important people. He uses them, their inner spirit, to speak to my inner spirit. It is a calling forth in my response to active love and compassion for His chosen people and praise of His creation.

These stories are not a spiritual programme. Each has its own individual thrust evoking a response from the reader. I suggest one ponders them silently; allows them to speak in the depths of their being. His word is a "two edged sword" which cuts through much of the fabric of our inner being. We experience an ever-penetrating insight into our hidden recesses.

The light of his spirit penetrates our darkness. If we say "Yes" it illuminates it with his glow of light - Light Divine.

Then one day the creator and creature will be one as we praise his name forever. Deeply amid the murmurings of your heart, you await the Master's touch. You reveal the hidden treasures at the touch of His hand. Darkness becomes light, secrets, gently revealing the splendour of the Master's touch.

Life on the Ocean

The sea looks vast, so vast that it speaks of unlimited depths, depths which cannot be seen by the naked eye. "How vast are you?" Asks the little child. "Do you ever take off your cloak so I may see you?"

The sea was silent. Its presence spoke of stories untold. It told of its expanse of travel and the many countries it surrounded. It told of the many ships that sailed its waves. These were ships of many images - liners, cruisers, merchant sailing ships, war ships. Each had its own story and its own history; each a history known only to its owner, an unknown history!

Oh, if only these ships would speak! What would be revealed? Stories of hunger and thirst; stories of love and laughter; stories of pain and joy - all silently chronicled in its bows.

A young man came along. He too gazed at the sea. It spoke to him of adventure and faraway, interesting places. Perhaps more interesting than his own land he thought. Oh to be there! He stood; he gazed and then moved on.

An elderly lady came sometime later. She too stopped and gazed. Pensive thoughts unfolded. Her life lay before her like a carpet unrolled on the vast ocean of life. She sat, she thought, long lost thoughts of many years. Like the ships she had sailed the ocean of her life. Her story wasn't all known. Much was locked in the vast treasure box of her heart. She sat. These thoughts had been silent, perhaps dead, many years. Better not turn the key on that treasure box she thought, or did she call it just a box? Yes, perhaps box was better - it was simply of no value. "Keep it hidden that is best", said a voice within.

She sat and sat. Little by little the key of the box turned slowly. She was not turning it. No, a power beyond her was gently moving her to gaze no longer at the sea but at the depths of the sea within her. "I will get up and walk", she said to herself. "That will keep me from pondering. Then I will not be calling out of their silence so many thoughts, so many events of my life. Yes keep going, what is the point? Don't stop", her mind was saying. But deep within her there was a cry; a cry for release, a cry for light, a cry to open up and let the fresh invigorating air of the sea within her enliven her.

In a way she felt captivated. There was no letting go now. Her heart had taken possession of her life. A freedom **to be** was being evoked in her as she gazed on her journey through the sea of life.

A smile pierced her lips. Her face relaxed, joy sprang up in her being. Why, what was she experiencing now? She was in another spin but not one of turmoil. No, it was one of joyful hope.

She sat. Her story unfolded before her. Amazing lightness flooded her heart. She experienced another presence lifting the sadness and pain as she allowed the light to shine on her story.

It was like a dream. The depths she feared to look at were exposed. One by one her stories came to life. She beheld a vast treasure chest of joy, love and hope that was priceless. The key turned within her heart.

The hand that turned it was becoming more familiar to her. She sat and gazed at the wealth within.

A GLOW OF LIGHT

- Dare to gaze at the ocean box deep within you and allow the treasures to be revealed to you.
- Allow the word to speak to you in your heart.

Scripture Reflection: 2 Cor. 4-7

We are only the earthenware jars that hold the treasure, to make it clear that such an overwhelming power comes from God and not from us.

Lord, you know the depths of my sea. The treasures within my pain and joys are your gift to me. Thank you for leading me to salvage such treasures. May they cause me to praise you. Amen.

Wonder of Wonders

It was a dark summer's night; the mist had deepened and enveloped the view of the distant island. People read the message – time to take shelter! Gradually the shore was free of people. The darkness descended, a storm seemed imminent. One could read the sense of disappointment on their faces; their leisure time was being interrupted. Their physical well-being was deprived of the challenge of a long embracing walk. Perhaps this is what happens in life! The summer of brightness lasts only for a short time: radiant sunshine to both the tired body and mind, even shorter. Then the visitation of a storm, with its electrifying effects, hits through the life within. Someone sees a little house on the side of the cliff. The storm's threatening effects become less terrifying. There is a shelter, a comforting thought. They hasten their steps and the nearer they come to the house the more wonderful it appeared. Yes, there is a light within! Somebody is there – or is there?

The storm broke, torrential rain, fork lightening made their presence felt. Somehow they coped with each new step giving new energy. Aware of this they continued on the road. The light grew brighter too. It had a welcome in its rays.

They realized, as they finally made their last steps, that this was no ordinary house. Yes, they stopped to view it again, lit up by the fork lightning. It seemed unthreatened. It was made of granite stone like the dividing walls in the fields. It had been built by a master builder who knew his stones, how to cut them and place them. They fitted like a hand in a glove, close to each other. They radiated strength and spoke no word; no voice was heard. That was their power. The seeker sought their welcome, their warmth, as they entered the open door. Yes, there was somebody present there, at home there, but they could not see anybody. "Is this important?" They thought. "I only need to shelter. Then I will be on my way again, that is after the storm. How long will it last?" They asked themselves. No clear answer came to mind, maybe an hour! They entered and sat down. Peace reigned.

Through the windows there was a panoramic view of the seashore from on high. The cliff seemed to add to the beauty of the sea. They seemed so much at one with each other. Suddenly their eyes beheld a most beautiful rainbow, a full bow. Its strong rays of blue, red, yellow, orange, indigo and purple were suspended over the sea. Their eyes were captivated by it. They seemed to draw them to it. Wonder of wonders, its beauty filled the sky. If I were an artist I would paint it, they murmured to themselves, or if I had a camera, I would take a photograph of it; capture it forever!

At that moment their inner voice whispered, "Capture it for ever – how?" The wonder of the world cannot be captured, curtailed or embodied in paper. Its power is untouchable and incomprehensible. They stopped mid-stream in their thoughts and were lulled into contemplation. The presence within the house became a reality within themselves: creation and creator become one in the depths of their being.

A GLOW OF LIGHT

- Contemplate the storms of life you have experienced and their impact upon you.
- You are the Indwelling Presence of the Holy Spirit.

The Lone Voice

Sounds, sounds and more sounds were heard, voices hushed in the background. The atmosphere is tense with expectations. What is afoot? The road has been blocked for a long time now. What is happening at the further end of the street - a meeting, a protest or a gathering of neighbours? Time will tell! Then a lone voice is heard encouraging the people to take part in a peaceful protest. The cause was the unsocial conditions of the neighbourhood. The authorities seem blind, or are they are unwilling to acknowledge a need? The people must respond themselves. They are intent on what he is saying – nothing can be achieved in sleeping circles. Action must speak out their human cry for help. Many lives are at stake, particularly the young and the vulnerable elderly. These have no other voice to raise up their cause. They are the marginalised of society. Authorities do not see them as their greatest asset. Response is often at a snail's pace. Cheers go up, heads nod in agreement with the speaker. He, by the way, is of an age to have a foot in both camps. He has personal experience of their needs.

Then the crunch came. What action would they take and, most important of all, who was willing to stand up and be counted? Great causes always began, he told them, with people; people willing to face situations, even if the way ahead was not clear. Visionaries, he said, often get lost in the dream. They need action now.

The cheers and applause grew somewhat less enthusiastic. A more sombre sound echoed down the street. Were they going to drift away, one by one, in slow motion? Suddenly the interlude was broken by a faint nervous voice calling for action. No, it was not the speaker's voice, just one of the crowd, one who had listened to his message, had heard it, and somehow felt compelled to respond. "Where are the rest of you going?" He asked. "Home is it and forsake the cause of these people? No we can't do that. Come let us join hands in neighbourhood support. Let us commit ourselves to action, even if we do not know the way".

An eerie silence descended on the night air. It was a protesting silence and one could feel it in their bones. It radiated through the street and came to rest upon the crowd.

Crowds come and crowds go like sound but this crowd remained in pensive silence. The urgency of their invitation was gripping them. A calm, strong, controlled voice spoke. "The date of the next meeting will be ------." There was a silent hush. Was there a way out now? "Sign on here now, all those who wish to attend and start the roller coaster ride to initiate a way forward". More silence followed.

Ten minutes later and the roller coaster ride had started with spirited people aboard. The wheel had been turned on by the quiet, convinced voice of one person.

The rest of the story remains to be told.

A GLOW OF LIGHT

- What are the sounds you hear coming down your road?
- How are you responding to the call?

> O that today you would listen to His voice,
> Harden not your hearts.
>   Psalm 95: 7-8

The Flora and the Fauna

The sheet of ice spread across the road. The way was impassable to either foot or vehicle. "How does one take off from here?" asked the traveller.

It had been a wonderful holiday here in the glen; a quiet, remote and unspoilt valley. Few knew of its existence beyond the natives. It was so remote and confined in area, it did not merit a place on the map of this country. Definitely there would be no mention on a world scene. Yet there was something strange, perhaps unique, in its breath. One loved it, inhaled it but could never name it. Was this place of this world at all? People had often spoken among themselves about it. It was home to them and few ever wanted to leave it for far off shores.

My stay had been accidental. I was travelling in search of a place that would speak to me. By the way, I am an artist. That is how I came upon it and set up tent. I say tent because I felt enveloped in its atmosphere. The hills called out to me, the lakes invited me to linger. What of the flora and the fauna, so delicate in the wind that shone forth in the sunshine? Even the rain enhanced them. Its drops seemed to settle like jewels on the leaves.

This was a land that caused no stir. The hills stood steadfast. The lake held its silence and the flora knew its seasons - when to enrich the landscape; when to be non-intrusive, in sympathy with the decaying earth. Was it really decaying or letting its energy seep into the soil to regain its own unique strength and silently appear some months hence and captivate its admirers by just being flora?!

I had sat and walked during these months; allowed "The Valley", as the natives called it, to seep into my being. It awakened depths unseen before in me. They seemed to hold my hands, mix my paint and oils accordingly and then cause my hand to move across the canvas. At times I seemed not necessary. They were creating their own image in a way I could never do. People came and watched, gazed and asked about my technique. I felt lost for words. My technique - it wasn't mine! I invited them, too, to sit and allow the valley unfold its purpose. Some understood others passed on. They too were "free" travellers on this road.

Yes, the months have been long and short, dark and full of sunshine. I have made many new friends and learnt a little of the true meaning of tranquillity and hospitality, a hospitality I had not experienced from nature before.

Yes, at 10am today I was to leave "The Valley". My experience was over and new lands called within me. I say 'was to leave' but I am still here. Nature once again in its own unobtrusive way has spoken to me. A road glazed in ice is not an inviting road. It is like a flashing light proclaiming danger. TO BE AVOIDED is the message. I read the sign and listened to its warning. I don't know when or if I will ever move from here but I suspect the creator of ice will beckon me on - even further along the road.

A GLOW OF LIGHT

- Gaze at your valley and hear its silent call.
- Be still in His Presence and ponder His Word in 'Eyes of Wonder'.

Eyes of Wonder

Life is mine.
Do you know what life is?
Life is being one with me.

The journey may be hidden,
The way wearisome,
But you travel it,
Travelling at my pace.

There is no hurry,
The landscape is wide open.
It takes a gentle pace,
The pace of a traveller in search of wonder.

Do you wonder and ponder?
The road will be just road if you don't
You will be blind to the view.
The hills will be distant and unnoticed.

Travel the road with eyes of wonder.
Wonder is limitless.
There is no time length in its path.
Search for wonder deep within you.
It grows silently and calmly.
Amen.

The Castle by the Bridge

It is a beautiful picture unfolding. The artist sits by the ruins of an old castle at the foot of the bridge. The castle has been there for many centuries now, at least two centuries. It had been built by the dedicated hands of unrewarded labour. There is a plaque with the date 1749 inscribed on it but no mention of the men who bore the brunt of the heat to build it. Yes, it had a very definite purpose.

Tales abound of marauders and invaders. The people must be safeguarded against the gruesome tales becoming a reality in their lives. Yes, there was a lookout at each side of the castle, and a moat. This was important. If unexpected invaders got that close they would be drowned. This was unlikely to happen, though, as the view from the outlook points sent "search lights", lights of guards, over the extending fields.

Local history does not recall an invasion, not even an attempted one, but the castle is a grim reminder of what might have been! Today the plaque gives it its importance in the annals of time. Its fabric shows the wear and tear of the years. Winds have swept across it and its masonry is in need of repair. It is decision time for those in charge. Let it crumble and fall into ruins or invest in its reconstruction.

Plans keep shifting, being postponed and brought to the table again. Redrafting takes place. Where is the action? It is not action, it is delaying tactics that are occupying their minds. Does anyone really want the castle to have its rightful place again? Yes and no is the answer. It would be lovely to view it, have it as an attraction spot for visitors and tourists.

The returned exiles would recount many moments spent as children in its prestigious walls. The man who has travelled the world studying castles and historic buildings will be enthralled at its structure. Profits could be made from its "Opening Hours". Yes it is, or could be, valuable again.

The scene has changed though. Formerly it was a defence point; now the emphasis is on profit. Economic boom! How quickly the wheels within the drawbridge have turned. Yet, they seem to be grinding to a halt, choked also by the weed and overgrowth, cultivated by the delaying tactics of its guardians.

The castle stands silent but its walls speak out over the landscape. It has a mind of its own. It was built for a purpose by dedicated people. It sends out a cry from deep within its precinct "Come to my aid; don't let me fall apart. I have a purpose in life. Listen to me. See the splendour I could be. Can you imagine how I can enhance this land by my presence? I hear your plans. I sit in on your discussions. To me you lack commitment, a true commitment to my life. Lip service will not save me."

The way forward for you is clear. Take the risk involved, walk the bridge of my moat and grasp the challenge. You will be able to estimate the value of my presence across the world. Its influence will be great upon even those who never visit me. Risk, risk is the name of the game.

A GLOW OF LIGHT

- Take a walk around your castle.
- Hold a conversation with it about how it feels and the care it requires.
- What risks is it asking you to take?

Scripture Reflection: Matt. 13: 45-46

The kingdom of heaven is like a merchant looking for fine pearls; when he finds one of great value he goes and sells all he has and buys it.

Lord so often the echo of my castle goes out over the plains and I just allow it to go unheeded. May I peacefully have the courage to see the condition of my fortress and not fear any invasion; to risk your healing touch on my weak structures.

Electrified Railways

Electrified railways now speed along what was once fertile, arable land. It produced crops that fed the masses and could have, even in times of famine. Progress changed all that, the railroads captured the imagination of the engineers. This was the way forward. It heralded a new era of mass communication throughout the land and across the world.

The steel plated lines and sleepers, cut from the trees, were mounted along the wayside. Work was to begin. People were to be taken into the next century and many more to come. Rumours of the plans spread rapidly.

Like all news it struck deep into the hearts of the people. Opinions were for and against. What was becoming of the land? The four-year rotation system of crops would be no more. Life was changing but would it be for the better!?

One farmer remained silent but watched each new development of the plans pensively. The old days were hard. All depended on the weather but they had their merits. Alone in the fields one became aware of the returning seasons, the new blades of grass, the seeds of corn and the reaping of the hay.

It had a rhythm of its own. It was called into being like the rising sun and the going down of same. Yes, it would be an end of an era, sadly.

For others, thoughts of railways conjured up memories of trains puffing along the mountain sides singing their own songs to the beat of "I will, I won't make it" as it laboured up the hills and children watching at the station for its arrival. Then the activity would begin; the filling of water and the stoking of fires. Its power would come from the earth, the very source they were now about to violate. Was it right to embark on such a development or is it a violation of people's rights to preserve their heritage, their land, their homesteads?

Years have passed. Life all around has uprooted itself and presented a new focus for people. Industrialisation has become the key word of the living society. The steam train, in its turn, has been quietly and with little opposition removed. It is now the Age of Improvement. Inventions, like the seasons, not only have a beginning but also an end.

The electric trains are here to speed along. Alas the rail lines are not at one with them! They too are not designed or sufficiently updated to welcome the high-speed technology.

The lines and the carriages, together with the engines, have different expectations of each other; expectations which cause friction of movement. The carnage scenes of crashes and derailment speak of the "power" of friction, however well it is clothed in a robe of progress. The road ahead for progress is wide open. Will it be progress?

A GLOW OF LIGHT

- What are the challenges, in the name of progress, that present themselves in your life?
- What elements could blur your vision?

Scripture Reflection: Book of Wisdom 7: 7-9

And so I prayed, and understanding was given me.
I entreated, and the Spirit of Wisdom came to me.

The Song of the Bird

A little bird sat on its perch. It was a young ash tree that one day would become an instrument and at the same time the willing ingredient of its sculptor. Its future was in the hands of humanity. It would provide shelter, work, joy and pleasure depending on the eye of the beholder. Its roots were deep. It had been planted with the loving care of its owner to produce ash trees for generations to come.

Yes people walked around it, sat under it and little ones attempted to climb it. It was fortunate, not like other trees that were vandalized and their lives cut short. Ecology and belief in this tree were strong influences in the mind of its owners. They considered it a privilege and treasure in the shady nook of their garden.

Oh yes, they had other trees. This was not an isolated tree bereft of companionship. It had good natural and social surroundings. It would be carefully tended and even some of its autumn leaves would be pressed for preservation. The Christmas festival would also highlight its place of honour. It would be used, in the proper sense, to adorn the house and hail in the living spirit of festivity.

In some unique way the purpose of this tree was being fulfilled. It was creatively proclaiming the birth of its creator amid the celebrations. It too echoed its glory. It was in tune with its planter where love of nature and its preservation sang their song of thanksgiving for the beauty and solace of nature.

I mentioned that little bird. It was perched on the top branch, monarch of all it surveyed. I gazed on it and my mind was captivated by the old phrase - a bird's eye view! Its eyes were so small that a pair of binoculars was necessary if one wished to look at it straight in the eye. Yet the power of that little, somewhat hidden, eye was immeasurable to the passer-by. It had a hidden power to penetrate into the world of nature around it. What was the view from its perch? It has not disclosed this to any human being. Its secret is wrapped in the mystery of its nature. How I wondered what its eye could see! It had a mind of its own, one I could not penetrate.

The wind rose and the branches of the ash swayed in its course. One expected it would either be blown off or fly for shelter. But no, it tenaciously held on as if enjoying the sway. The storm had no grip on it. Rather, it had a grip on its perch secure as monarch of all it surveyed. It radiated confidence – an inner strength in its tiny wee body. What was its source of strength I wondered? The message it conveyed was NO STORM WILL ROCK ME.

What of that unique and indelible red breast - a seal upon its breast since birth? It was no ordinary trademark. Folklore has its own revelations on that – the drops of blood that flowed upon it were sacred. It is one of the chosen people, keeping alive the memory of The Crucified One. This was no mighty bird in the eyes of the world, yet it sat upon the world scene with a ken unfathomable and a role of constant reminder of a loving God.

As an ambassador what did this role entail? There certainly is no job description drawn up. No, the little red breast just had to be! This is somewhat just like the ash tree. Just Be - a robin on an ash tree, that is fulfilment!

I often recall the two "creatures" of creation and wonder at the presence of their silence and its power. There is no proclaiming from the treetop who they are. Both are in their own way deeply rooted!

A GLOW OF LIGHT

- What salient points in this story challenge you?
- How rooted are you?

Scripture Reflection: Matt. 6: 26-29

Look at the birds of the sky ……. Your Heavenly Father feeds them.

Penetrating the Skies

Have you ever thought of how fascinating an aeroplane is? It takes off and soars up into the sky. I watched it one day. On the ground it was not very exciting to look at – just metal! It was a wet and windy day, one that did not enhance the object before us.

I am sure Michelangelo looked down from his heavenly abode and thinks to himself, "I had plans for making one". People still refer to his drafts as adventurous, imaginative; but how far-fetched and unrealistic they are! Plans have been drawn up over the centuries. The sketches build up upon each other, each with its own variation, modification and streamlining. The sizes develop, one seater, flying like a kite amid the blue sky and seeking its hidden course behind and above the clouds. The Concord stands quite close by, what a sight to behold, its streamline nose ready to break the sound of the speed barrier.

Control towers signal the take off at last. The air is clear. The mighty bird is empowered by a machinery of uncountable parts and an army of screens and instruments, each finely pin pointed to guide it into and on heavenly course.

The passengers are an interesting group to watch. There is the young couple; he is tall, slim and has had a fair share of the sun. They laugh and chat, thoroughly relaxed. This is but yet another step on their world tour. Theirs is a dream adventure, to be recounted to many starry-eyed friends later. Then there is the young mother, aided by Concord staff, with her two young children. They seem quiet in

33

spirits, while on her face a picture of sadness appears. What is her story? It is hard to say, but there is great pain enwrapped in her expression. They pass through the barrier and their story goes with them.

Then there is a group of four, definitely refugees. They are unobtrusively, but very deliberately, being escorted to the plane. The end of their journey - and of life: who knows? There were many others, a plane full, even politicians, with the course of the world in their hands. What decisions will they ever make: radical, conservative or just simply middle of the road? - the future of the world in their hands and they appear to carry it lightly!

The blades of the plane burst into rotation. The very life of the engines is empowered to do what no human being can do - reach to the heavens. No one, save those who are motivated to be shot into space in the hope of discovering another planet and its possible space folk!

The plane has vanished into the air. The passengers and crew have a "life" up there, unseen by the human eye on terra firma. The mighty bird is suspended in air, held only by the refined tuning of instruments. A risk, a challenge – what is it? Can we read the mind of the pilot who feels an urgent wish within him to carry his plane, his passengers into the unknown? Yes, the wonder he beholds around him defies explanation. He remains silent on its wonders. Then his lone mechanical voice speaks – 70,000 feet high, winds, tail winds, estimated time and temperature on arrival ----. Interesting facts or are they? Why is he so silent on the wonder about him? I wonder why! Perhaps one day he too will put a voice on his experience as he soars high on his heavenly flight.

A GLOW OF LIGHT

- Consider the many people, known and unknown who are on life's journey with you.
- What wonder does this flight through time evoke in you?
- How does the role of the pilot speak to you?

Scripture Reflection: John 14, 2-3

I go to prepare a place for you,
And after I have gone and prepared you a place,
I shall return to take you with me.

Emotions or Wisdom

The cars sped along the dual carriageway at 70 miles an hour. The nearer they approached the underpass the flashing speed board gave warnings – SLOW DOWN 40 miles per hour. It flashed and they sped on. The urgency of their travel became the determination to keep going and this blinded their reason to the legal process. Where were they all speeding to? What was their raison d'être, or did they even know? They were all Eight on the Enneagram and felt quite at home. The few motorists, with conscious awareness, braked and became an obstacle to the speedy "entertainers" of the road. In a very tactful way they caused the "fliers" to speak sweet words, at least silently about them, while they forged ahead. The legal minded, true to their wish to obey, drove in direct contrast. Both were motivated by their inner source of emotions!

What about the One - The Perfectionist? The car was shining with a polish of elbow grease. I am not sure if it was their own elbow grease or that of the valet centre down the road. The roof of the car was rolled back, the inside was immaculately dressed as was its owner. They decried the dust of the road, which clothed many of the passing cars. "Wouldn't you think they would give it a wash if not a polish", they silently murmured and added, "How can they exist in such conditions?" And so the story of the road unfolds!

On another occasion I was in my car and in a most professional way, or so I thought, had reversed my 10-year old "limousine" into a parking space. It was a side street with one- way traffic restrictions. At that moment there was no other moving traffic on the road. Just as I turned the wheel to finally straighten up it happened! I have heard of "neighbours from hell"; this was a woman, from where I do not know! I saw no approach on her part or, for that, no departure. I witnessed, as from another world, this human being inside my car. It was her verbal barrage that woke me up to reality. I was at that moment the innocent victim of verbal road rage.

The door slammed closed and I was left stunned. Who was she? Where did she go? I don't know. Am I the only person that day to have experienced her emotions? I don't know. She stills remains for me the "unknown woman" of the road rage. In kind of a strange way I came through the experience alone on a side street – a street that only went one way! I too had only one way to go; continue on my mission to talk about the Love of God to a group waiting to ponder it! The contrast was startling. What were my emotions calling? I am not sure I knew then. I do know now!

Oh, the joys of motoring invented by man for man (and woman)! What are those joys? Is it the reality painted so often by the advertisements that clog our screens – and minds? I wonder why they do. I wonder why! Will the light ever dawn and penetrate our reasoning? Reasoning, what is that? Is it the ability to see through the blurred screen of our minds and to perceive our interaction with our inner self, as we drive along the motorway of our life's journey?

A GLOW OF LIGHT

- Emotions and reasoning can all too often be at odds within us.
- How comfortable are you with them?
- LORD, teach us the wisdom of your ways.

The Gift of Knowing

My God, do I know you?
How can I know the depths of your Being?
Your love alone proclaims your greatness,
Greatness which never ceases to amaze.

Amazement is of you.
It enlightens our minds,
Provides food for our thoughts
And life for our journey

Teach us to be still Lord,
To touch in some small way
The edge of your fountain of wisdom.

Wisdom gladdens the heart.
It reveals your love,
It reveals our love for you,
Poor as we are.

Guide us Lord on our journey.
The days are long,
The days are short,
But meeting you is the priceless gift.
Gift of the moment,
Gift of each day;
Teach us to see the gift;
The gift of ourselves
Your gift to your world,
Unworthy though we be.
We are gifted,
Gifted to proclaim your love.
Gifted to let your gift be gift to others.

The Slot Machine

The slot machine moved into action. It seemed like a mechanical world of metal sound as we passed by on the pier head. It was dull to look in at in spite of the neon lights flashing like some great warning procedure. Yet it was these lights that drew something deep within us to penetrate its "sanctuary". I say "sanctuary" for it had hidden depths reaching out to the people who entered it. The sound of metal, handles being pulled, silver dropping down chutes, above all the heavy din of the copper, all attracted the watcher.

Which machine do I take over or does this machine take me over? That is the big question! My mind boggles; is that question too profound to be even asked, thought the old lady, though not so old! Folks there knew her as Megan, a regular customer.

Yes, she was well dressed in a casual way, in keeping with the latest summer trend. She seemed alert. In a way she was a dab hand at pulling that handle! The oranges and lemons rolled round and always seemed to stop in a correct line. The flow of cash began to slide down the chute. Her eyes laughed at it while her hands gratefully collected their reward.

She counted it enthusiastically as if it was her life's savings. Then into the bucket they went only to be quickly inserted into the equally grateful machine, claiming its own property back. She looked at the other machines. Was the one in the far corner more generous to its investors or more grabbing she wondered. Pensive glances went across the floor!

Suddenly her tip-toes went lightly across the floor. She took possession of her new entertainer or was it an entertainer? This was certainly not her first time trying it. She approached it with a sharp keen eye, like a bird of prey ready to pounce and feast off its catch.

She was a slim little lady, not the kind if you met her at the end of the pier that you would associate with the machines. But there was something about her this evening that indicated to the onlooker that this was a priority for her − part of her way of life! Again the noisy flow of the push of the handle and the money flushing through resounded. She knows her business, I thought. Where would I stand in the scale of ratings if I invested!

I sensed a deep reluctance within me. Many reasons came to mind; I had no change and I really didn't know how to use the machines. There was obviously great skill required. One needed to be au fait with the mind of the machine. Then there was the question of which one to try.

Yes, I was getting closer to a trial. My mind focused on which one. In my process of discernment I had advanced along the road of neon lights and metal machines. I, the person who didn't really appreciate this lady's activity, had one toe inside the camp now.

I had seen the lights and heard the clash of money. I was actually been captured and didn't realise it. I was aware of just some ideas floating through my mind. Were these ideas carrying me into a new venture? I didn't pause to think. At another level I was travelling into new territory with my eyes closed, while at the same time I was in a discerning process as the books say! I had advanced, I was at a crucial moment in my life. This was a moment never to come my way again. I said crucial, yes it was, I had to make a choice that could not be undone. That choice was now!

Gingerly I walked towards the less foreboding machine I saw. I slid the money down the chute; I had three different choices, I lost. I stopped, was I to venture again or? Deep within me a little voice seemed to say "DON'T GET HOOKED. MANY HAVE INNOCENTLY GONE DOWN THIS ROAD BEFORE YOU". I thought many have given all and lost all.

Their lives were at stake, not the hoard of cash in the well of the machine. It, the machine, was educated to preserve its stance in life. It was only fulfilling its purpose. I paused and stopped. Then, with an inner reserve, made my way out.

Outside I decided to stroll along the pier. It was a beautiful summer's night and as darkness descended I wondered at the inner darkness, and perhaps pain, that led so many to risk their lives on a machine. By the way Megan was still fully "Alive" in the grip of the metal as I departed.

A GLOW OF LIGHT

- The paths of life can be strange at times. Reflect on times when the glitter of your "neon light" captivated you.
- How did this change your life?

God, guardian of my rights, you answer my call.
When I am in trouble you come to my relief.
Psalm 4: 3

Teach me discernment and knowledge
For I trust in your commands.
Psalm 118

The Anniversary

It was mid-May. John, 84 years old, decided to go for his daily constitutional, that's if his legs would carry him. His youth was indeed spent. That is what his limbs were telling him anyway. But this May morning called him out of the seclusion of his flat to breathe in the fresh air of the countryside around him.

He recognised that he was lucky. He was still part of the countryside; the "big men" had not taken over the fields around him to replace the green grass and the chestnut trees, which perpetuated so much fun each year with their conkers. John remembered the fun and the joy of his youth. The conker matches were like a pop festival to the youthful ears of today.

He set out placing his stick and his feet in a careful rhythm along the path. To be able to touch the earth with his feet felt like an energising, new age treatment on the pressure points of his feet. Is this the effect one really feels from the spoiling touch of another person, he wondered. His steps get lighter and his head less light. He was experiencing a sense of well-being after those long months of feeling under the weather.

His heart was also light; hope pervaded his heart, hope of even better days to come. Who would have thought it could happen today! Today is a very special day for John. A day which was, sixty years ago a moment of true love. She was a girl, fair and beautiful to his eyes. He had known her for three years and then the knot was tied. Yes, it was love of all loves leading to even greater love. He remembered the spontaneous moment when he shyly asked her to be his love for life. He remembered the confidence he felt also. The secret of his confidence was – well didn't he know how much she loved him! Like every girl before, she had waited for this moment wondering when would the words gain possession of his lips. It happened.

Can you imagine it? They were walking quietly along the cliff top. The air was full of expectation. Suddenly he turned to her, clasped her hands and uttered the sacred words "Will you marry me, Dora?" Life was never the same again.

To neighbours they appeared like any other couple. They were blessed with little John, Eileen and Therese, the joys of their lives. Their laughter filled the house, tears were shed, first steps were taken and words spoken. He remembered them all now in the depths of his being. They were the moments that kept his spirits going now. Somehow they spoke to him of love given and love returned in abundance. Their photographs are always before his eyes too. They are his living treasure. His extended family – his beloved and cherished grandchildren are his pride and joy. Alas though his little John is married and living in Holland. Eileen is in California, but luckily for John, Theresa a social worker, lives near him. He is very proud of her obvious love and care of other people too. She is also the image of her mother!

Dora, long since dead is closer than ever to him. He recalls the day they chatted, watching the birds play in the pond in their garden, birds refreshed by the splashing of their wings. He remembers also her last words –"We must get some nuts for them." That was Dora, ever attentive to the needs of others and all creation!

John turned the corner of the path and went through the little wooden gate into Conker Walk. There, before his eyes, was an experience he had lived through many years ago. A mother sat peacefully relaxed on the grass, beside her two little boys. They were that wonderful age that invites exploration and activity.

One, about four years old, was quite engrossed in making his daisy chain, while she with arms around the two year old, lovingly twined his daisy chain for him. The love of a child and the wonder of creation were all one! John thought of all the days he had played with his children so long ago. He recalled how adventurous they were climbing the trees, jumping the walls, the cut knees, the lot! That was what made their lives so close knit. Nothing, not even old age could take these memories from him. They were his lifeline and he treasured them. They were like an old record that he took out and played so often. They were his priceless collection; they were his and always would be!

Yes, it was a lovely way to celebrate his anniversary. He would always keep alive the joy of that moment, a joy nobody could now take from him or relish it, as he did. Calmly now he walked on. He was very aware that generation after generation would be full of wonder at the sight of a delicate daisy, a daisy that reflected the true love of the God of creation.

A GLOW OF LIGHT

- Gaze with appreciation on the moments of joyful love in your life.
- What response does it evoke in you?

The Touch of Purest Love

God of power and glory,
Where is the creature
More loved than in your Heart?

How can this be Lord?
Amid a world of love and envy,
You stand alone
In purest love.

Teach us to love Lord.
Teach us to allow
Thy healing power to heal us.

Life is your gift,
Strong in love,
Wonderful in power.
Amen.

The Blue Print

The road ahead appeared to be long. We set out. Yes, it was going to be a long journey. One of my friends had suggested looking at a map some days previously. This was unknown territory to us and necessitated planning, meticulous planning as it turned out to be! Not content with the good old reliable atlas, but then again it may not be up to date, all attention turned to the web. WWW------- and, hi presto, the magic, hidden little encyclopaedia began to unravel the information. Minutes later it instructed us to "press for print". This was to be the blue print of our journey – at least on paper! We studied it diligently and frequently till the route became imprinted on our minds. A sense of security prevailed; the web had spoken!

Our attention then turned to, well guess what? You are right! Food, welcome food, took over our attention. What did we want or was it what was required for the journey to keep the body and soul together! No, we were not stopping to be "greased" up by fast foods. Ours was going to be a healthy, relaxing picnic in keeping with the excellent itinerary of a map, produced by you know who! Brown bread headed the list, followed by the salads, refreshing cucumber and cherry tomatoes, crowned by delicious slices of smoked salmon This was to be enhanced by a glass of wine to refresh the system! It was hot weather and the question of who would drive came up. The lot fell on Tony. He volunteered to have a low calorie drink.

We had booked our hotel right by the edge of the sea and its sandy beach cove. The Royal Yacht Club was well known for its cuisine and hospitality.

Renowned for its chef, it drew folks from far and near. This was going to be our treat to ourselves. What could be better than this resort – and the desire to treat ourselves! Days of leisure, rest and golf thrown in with sailing. Everything was falling into place. The road ahead was long. That too would be part of the enjoyable holiday, free from mobile phones and faxes, that we had promised ourselves.

Tony sat behind the wheel. By the way, the car was a new speedy dark blue, and one could say it was about to embark on its maiden voyage. Two hours later we pulled up in a quaint little village by the shore of the lake. It was time for a walk to keep the cramps off and aid circulation, followed by a restful cappuccino. Yes, it was to be cappuccino all round. The froth of its milk, like foam, was refreshing to our lips! Then the urge to get going again came upon us. We had a long way to go and we would need to stop again, for, don't forget, the picnic!

We packed into the car. The engine revved up and we set off. The windows were well down as we considered this more accommodating than the air conditioning, which after all only recycled the air, and did not refresh it. The stereo played The Trout by Schubert. We were enthralled: pastoral scenes before us and pastoral music in our ears. This was heaven. Maybe we were heaven bound! Oh, I forgot to mention that we were well protected against motorways, we just travelled along the quiet country roads. Shortly, we met the truck! It was huge and, as it approached, in a flashing moment seemed to be warning us that it owned and ruled the road. It came straight for us, hit us full on and turned to "slide down" the side of our car, tumbled and regained its balance. Finally it ended up in the ditch on its own side of the road. Its "joy ride" was for about three hundred meters. We hadn't to stop. We were forced to! The journey had come to an abrupt end. Tony sat stunned. The three of us Michael, my husband, and Joan, Tony's wife, cried out, but there was nobody to hear us – or so it seemed. Alone, all alone, we thought of our heavenly journey and nobody dared mention it to the other!

Tony was first to speak. "What condition is the truck driver in?" he asked. The men went to investigate cautiously. We looked back. We noticed their faces seemed to relax as they turned in our direction. He was alive, unharmed but shocked! Somehow our long journey had ended. The picnic was over and we longed to return home. What a longing amid fright – just to be where one really belonged and touch, with a different attitude, the old familiar things. Above all to be reunited with those who loved us most. A journey had begun; a journey had ended and what an experience!

A GLOW OF LIGHT

- How planned, and controlled, is your journey through life?
- What insights have you gained by pondering your story and how does "letting go" touch you?

Lead us Lord.
Open our eyes Lord to the wonder of your paths
And the banquet prepared for us.

Mid Ocean

The boat shuddered. We swayed while the warmth of the sunshine enveloped our shoulders through the lookout viewpoint of the ship. It was a calm crossing but now we were riding on the big swell in mid ocean. It was an August morning and this was depicted in the folks around us.

We had one of those corner window seats with full view of the passengers aboard. It was a seat that often found it became a haven for tired bodies. Right beside me a husband is stretched out, fast asleep, in what appears to be a very uncomfortable position. Maybe it is not so for him as he is one that is revived by his forty winks!

Beside the little round table his wife is seated. Her strength and comfort comes from a cuppa, yes of coffee, and wait for it – well you know the answer! A big bar of Fruit and Nut chocolate is being tenderly assassinated by her tender hands, at odd intervals. Meanwhile, she is engrossed in the daily tabloid. The news of the day has its own headlines. How often it can be heeded by its millions of readers as gospel!

At the far end of the lounge the priceless Big Box has taken up its position – a permanent one. Faces are glued to it; some Wild Western, with all that that entails, is the source of life for its onlookers. Its voice is only dimmed a little by the continual chatter of the occupants of other seats.

There is also a family gathering in one central area. They are obviously ending what appears to have been a most enjoyable holiday in a "foreign" land. A land not so foreign to many of the passengers! They, nature can tell, were born of its fresh air and beauty of historic culture. Oh the family, that is the elders, have counted and neatly placed their little piles of euros, their "leftovers", on the newspaper in front of them. It looks like a little poker table with all that might entail for the fortune of this chosen few!

That is what I thought, but there has been a further development. A group of teenage daughters, of the renowned adults, are now counting the fortune they have each received from their respective parents. One calls, "Dad, I got four euros". A smile lit up the dad's face. He had given joy to her and he, by her enthusiastic reception of this mighty fortune, has received so much joy in return from her happiness. I pondered as I watched – a little gift, so insignificant, creating so deep a joy. I thought a lot about that and my mind was led down many avenues!

Then there was the highlight of my journey. My inner being cried out for food. No, not the simple food of kindness but food to nourish my long fasting or what felt like long fasting! Our day had begun early. The car had hit the road shortly after 6am.

That too was an interesting time of the day. Most creatures seemed still in their bunks, or perhaps were considering taking a major leap onto the floor, to hail in the new day. I gazed at the sky, the misty dew was rising over the sea at the south side. Then suddenly the wonder of creation, the silent rising sun, gave a thrill to my being. Its splendour and silence deserved a mark of respect. My hands were on the wheel so my gesture had to be from within! The car, with its four wheels, could drive with deep respect under the umbrella of this rising sun.

As for my inner call to food! I can't resist it. Didn't He who gave me the splendour of nature also give me the call to food? The Emporium of food on board offered great choices. I walked around. The whiff of the cuisine, in one area, was enough to make me pass through it without delay! Something more palatable was what my delicate system required, or so I told myself! Even the Delicatessen counter didn't entice me. Finally, I decided to treat myself and to go the whole hog. It was a "light" breakfast, the one they say "start the day with". This would give me a wholesome start to what was to be a most pleasant journey. What was to come in the course of the day remained unknown, but just now I felt well done to! I decided to lounge in its comfort and let the ship, guided by the captain, do his work! My enviable task was to sit back and let the world sail by. Oh, Happy Day!

A GLOW OF LIGHT

- What facets do you observe in the mid-ocean of your day-to-day life?
- How present are you to them?
- What are the avenues of your life that you avoid revisiting and why?
- What inner food do you crave for?

Lord for to-morrow's food I do not long.
Teach me to be nourished by the present, the gift of the present moment.

The Unknown Woman

A woman sat silently in the pew. She had come to church, as she did daily for Mass. To her surprise it was a funeral mass. She didn't know anyone in the parish had died. A strange feeling came over her. "Who is dead? Why hadn't somebody mentioned the death to her?" she wondered. No, it was not that she had to know all the news of the locality, but this was different. In a way it seemed special. She waited in wonder. Margaret was a kind lady who would have reached out to anyone in need.

I arrived near the church. Oh, it was different for me. I was a visitor, a stranger, just passing through today. As I approached I heard the sound of music echoing from the church. My reaction was instant – oh, not a funeral! It was a glorious day and I was caught up in the burning heat, enjoying myself in a relaxed way. A funeral did not really, at that moment, fit my bill. I approached the door, a little squeak, and I was in.

The priest stood at the top, in front of the altar. He too, took part in the singing of "How Great Thou Art". Then I saw the coffin, plain and simple, no flowers adorning it. Everything seemed hushed. The priest spoke. His voice melodiously led us into a farewell to Kathleen. He sprinkled the coffin with holy water reminding us of her Baptism. Yes hers, whoever she was! That done the white cover was slowly and carefully placed over the coffin. The latter seemed to come to life now. It had a new appearance of hope about it. He, Fr. John, told us it was to remind us of new life. Yes, her new life. She had what we all hope will be.

Religiously the server placed the crucifix on the cloth. Two lives seemed to become one at that moment. Kathleen and the symbol of her creator were lying side by side! The impact was powerful and made doubly so by the Word of God, the Bible, placed beside the crucifix. Somehow it spoke to us of new life. The message was clear – the Cross and the Power of The Word were inseparable. Still, I asked, "Who was dead?"

The mystery of mysteries was about to be uncovered, or was it? Fr. John, in a very welcoming way, thanked us for coming to pray for Kathleen and to give thanks for her life. Oh, he knew we didn't know her; neither did he. He had actually never met her. His "duty" today was not, he said, to record all her life story and events but to thank God for her life, whatever it was and however long. The strangeness of her story grew. Nobody knew her, it seemed, except three or four people in the front row. Yes, he thanked them too for coming such a long way. "Where was that?" I thought. The statement only added to the mystery of Kathleen. My mind could not "root" her anywhere. How strange!

A look from over his glasses and he reminded us of our place. We were all strangers too, strangers to one another, gathered here, each for their own reason. He invited us to thank God for this woman. It was a poignant feeling. It sent a shudder through my bones.

What was Kathleen's story and where was she to be buried? I thought. What must her life have been like, that on this day there were only strangers there to thank God for her? Had she a family? What, oh what, caused a lone woman to be so alone! I thought of her life, had she any joy or simply the pain of the forgotten one? She perhaps, was one of the many forgotten people in our world. That may be the case but it evoked a reply within me, which said, "Kathleen had smiled to the end. She had kept her dignity, and He alone today, who knows her story, walked with her to the end of the road."

As I looked on her life I realised she had received all. A mighty banquet was prepared for her and she was present at it. The world of work and pleasure may go on. Kathleen had ceased to work and ponder. Now, she sang her Alleluia! She was not alone, though the strangers in the church remained strangers. The mystery of her life became more profound, while her Alleluia was in tune with her heavenly friends who welcomed her!

A GLOW OF LIGHT

- This is a simple story with a profound truth.
- How does your inner being respond to it?

Life

Life Eternal!
Life unpurchased by us,
Life.

The Greatness of the Moment;
The moment of our dying,
Is the immeasurable hidden secret,
A secret to behold as we come face to face
With the God of Love, our God.

Can the mind fathom this moment?
Can it put words on it?
No, death is beyond human experience.
It is the ultimate moment of knowing you, my God.

Who can fear it?
None, it is the total giving of Yourself to each of us,
finally.
Welcome is the amazing state that awaits us.
How finite we are in the face of this great mystery of
love!
Angels adore Him.
Mary implores Him.
We will be one in this profound adoration.
Minds cannot comprehend this glory to be shared
with us.
Faith alone believes what is hidden!
This is faith – belief in what we cannot make sense of.

In your wisdom Lord,
Carry us on the wings of faith in each earthly moment,
To that final moment of Love Divine.

Sudden Decision!

It is now 10 am and I am sitting here in a comfortable armchair. There is nothing unusual in that, save that as I awoke this morning and greeted in a new day from my bed. I had no idea of what the day had in store for me.

The first few hours were spent in the accomplishment of my usual programme. It takes me an hour to really come round, and realise that I am a thinking person. So often I feel just like a robot, but today I was even more so!

Now, I am not given to quick decisions, but maybe it was the lure of the sunshine which lured me out of my very reasonable mind! I say lured and reasonable mind, because I made a quick decision. So quick and decisive, that now eight hours later, I can hardly believe it myself.

You see, I had just returned from a holiday last night. It was a holiday with a difference, I may add. I suppose it was a change of location and occupation. Yes, I was by the sea and fortunately for my brother George, I was free to spend the time with him. I say fortunate; in his saner moments, he may not have called it fortunate! Yet these weeks were his time of need. He had need for some T.L.C. and a helping hand. By nature he is quite an independent person, but being human, he too has his moments of need. This time the cause and effect of his need was what is considered to be one of the outcomes of reaching old age! I am not sure when this stage of a person's life takes over. What I do know is that it shows itself in many forms. Some indications are – the aching bones, the less active mind, the loop system, not to talk of the chair, which, with a press of a button, takes one speeding down the road! The latter rings out its silent warning, "I am coming down the road, clear the pathway before me!" This has a power of its own, not to be taken lightly by the passer-by!

My brother, well, his ageing nature was calling out – my knee, oh, my knee! So, not unusual, he was offered a replacement knee. He really had no alternative if he wished to walk again. The news at the beginning sounded as if a mechanical man had entered our family. Four weeks later and he is now walking, not with his usual gait or four mile cruise each day, but he is on his feet, and that is no small wonder. The fragility of the human being was seen so many times in those weeks.

Where did this leave me, you might ask? Well I was nursemaid, housemaid and to the eyes of the onlooker – just a sister taking care of a loving brother. You ask, "What has all this to do with my speedy decision today".

As I said at the beginning, I had just returned from my new type of holiday, feeling very pleased that I had been of help to one in need. Then I began to hear my own need, a need to relax and breath in the indescribable and energising fresh air of South Wales. Within moments – half an hour, I had decided I was going to have my holiday. I was going to pack my case and go! I was stunned by my reaction to a sudden thought, or, was it an inspiration? Five hours later and I have arrived.

I say arrived, in more sense than one. I have arrived physically. I am among the Welsh Hills and the green pastures, all of which speak of health and beauty. But, I have also arrived at, a deeper moment in time and a deeper centre within my being. Freedom to listen and respond has been born within me today!

A GLOW OF LIGHT

- Reflect on what holds you back from moving through life, with a "free spirit"

Scripture Reflection: Isaiah 40, 31.

They that wait upon the Lord shall renew their strength.
They shall mount up with eagles' wings;
They shall run and not be weary;
They shall walk and not faint.

The Hay Wagon

The car sped along the road. It was a racer car, with the bonnet closed up; nothing could be seen of the occupant or occupants. They had a definite aim as they drove along, obviously to get ahead and waste no time with slow moving traffic. They edged in and out of the line as each moving car challenged them on their course. They, it appeared, were masters of the road ahead!

In front of me there was a dark blue car, with its lights on, in the mid afternoon's sunshine. Maybe they thought the latter would cancel out the radiant beam of sunshine, which passed through the windscreen! The driver was very cautious and had a sense of the road, or so it seemed. Suddenly my eyes caught sight of his tail-lights. Something I hadn't noticed before struck me with amazement; and if I may say so, filled me with agitation. "Watch it," I said to my friend. At each bend in the road the driver braked, and even if there wasn't a bend he braked. He was driving almost continuously, for the last ten miles, braking every few seconds!

To dampen my agitation I thought kindly – this is their first time on this road. A little feeling of pity gripped me as we drove on the edge of a sheer drop around the mountainside. The Black Mountains are awesome to behold, and even more awesome to drive by. Yet, many a person had driven this way before, and lived to tell the tale.

Heights and sheer drops, though not alien to me, are certainly not what I consider to be friendly and inviting landmarks of nature. Yet today, in some surprising way, they sent a thrill up my spine. Was it because I was actually enjoying myself driving, while somewhat reminiscent of my own fear and inadequacy of skill in combating the ups and downs of mountain terrain in the past! Surely it was good to feel, it was different now than in the past, or was it?

With that a "flying" car overtook the four of us, as we were gliding through the valley. It had business on hand; urgency was the note of its speed. We must have appeared like drivers from Mars who were used to having the whole planet to themselves, to cruise along. Urgency had not entered our vocabulary. Life appeared so different from our point of view. "Slowly does it," was our motto, "but not too slowly!"

Slowly, but how slowly, can you go? Our peaceful pace was suddenly halted when the hay-wagon, of freshly cut hay, intercepted our path and declared not only its right to be there but for it, too, to travel at its own pace along its familiar road home. I say travel, but this is probably an exaggeration of the word travel! Yet, it went along carrying its priceless load. It would be family income and bedding for the cattle. A noble career, even if it was an unostentatious one!

Somehow this humble vehicle, with its fruits of the soil, reaped by the strength of the farmer, was indicating to its followers no there was no right or left indication to be seen - just a persona of ease and diplomacy. To my surprise, I became aware that its diplomatic appearance was proclaiming a deep and sensitive message to other users of the road. The message read, "My humble appearance is precious to those who see me for what I am!"

I inhaled this profound message as I kept pace behind the wagon. I asked myself, "has this statement gone into my very system?"

A GLOW OF LIGHT

- What message do you proclaim as you drive through life?
- Does the image and message of the hay-wagon speak to, or challenge you, in any way?

The Gift of Me

Oh, immense Love of your little one!
You cherish me dearly,
Dearly as a precious stone.
All protection is mine.
No wind can blow me from my place.
A place you have given me in life;
A place unique, insignificant to many;
Wonderful gift of you to me!

Teach me to cherish my being,
To wonder at it,
To praise its creator
And sing songs of praise to you!

The Setting Sun

I watched the setting sun taking up its position and claiming the sky as its throne, over the hills tonight. It is, as so often described in every day terms, like a bowl of fire. It cast its hue over and beyond the ken of a human person.

Something wonderful was happening. The whole of creation was in unison with its Maker. Who had set this sunset in motion? Who had placed it to go to rest in the West? Different people, who passed along the road, and many other roads, would have different answers – and perhaps questions to ask! I looked and I saw its hues and read the signs of another summer's day tomorrow a day which would give us a feeling of light heartedness. Have you ever noticed the difference in people on a sunny day? The rays seem to touch the cockles of their hearts and gloom disappears, at least for a few hours!

I wondered at this sunset. It puzzled me because it refused to answer my questions! That to my unscientific mind was gruelling, perhaps like the man who always asks questions and expects an answer, even if it is not the right one! I remember the story of the man who asked a well-known saint, "When would he be free from the sin of the flesh?" He replied, "I am sure," with a satirical smile on his face, "three days after death!"

So it was tonight, the setting sun was not revealing any secret of its own history. Maybe I too have to wait till I have disappeared and rested beneath the setting sun in some quiet place! Then my resting will probably pose many questions to the passers-by. Like the tomb of the 'unknown soldier' in Westminster Abbey, they shall possibly stop, like all sightseers, and read the inscription! Not moved they shall continue on to the next headstone that catches the interest of their sightseeing eye. A thought has just struck me, what will be written on the stone – or will anything be?

Maybe it will be just a simple cross. That is an interesting observation of my own resting place. Somehow, already, preparations for it are quietly taken out of my control. Who will have the say? I don't really know! Does it matter where my sunset is? Placidly, as I write I say, "Not really." Will I always feel that way? I can't say! So the mystery of the setting sun has evoked in me thoughts of a crossing in my life, or is it a passing on? One I don't dwell on too often. I wonder why!

The answer possibly lies in a preoccupation with my quite interesting life, just now. Each day brings its own challenge: love, friendship, joy and pain. That fills the twelve hours that I am supposedly compos mentis. Everybody may not agree that I am but how do they know if I don't know myself! After all, as the wise old owl says, "I am the only one who knows how my mind functions!" That is a revelation to those who consider they do.

"From the rising of the sun to its setting," says the psalmist. I am just thinking what preoccupies the mind of the sun from its gradual blossoming into sight in the east to its time to sleep in the west? What is it thinking, or does it think, as it awakens billons of people to life and nurses others to sleep, as it closes their eyes with its paling light? Nation after nation around the world has been a recipient of its impact. Has it wondered at their response to it or is it too incapable of influencing our response to it? I pause and I think of my childhood days and the thrill of the setting sun over the Atlantic Ocean. So often we just sat and watched it.

The psalmist continues,
From the rising of the sun to its setting,
Praise be the name of the Lord!

This sun in all its moments of presence has called forth the praise of its Creator. What, I hesitate to wonder, has my rising and setting done to re-echo this call? That I will never know till I too am also three days beyond my final resting!

A GLOW OF LIGHT

- Are there questions in your life that seem to remain unanswered for you?
- Do you ever contemplate your setting sun and what word of wisdom would you wish your resting place to unfold to its passers-by?

Life Songs

Silent streams,
Gushing waters,
All portray the glory of Him.

Strength of beauty,
Calmness of creation,
Where is love more profound?

Mountains speak their story,
High praise of their Master,
Calling on all to sing
Their praise at noontide.

Stars shining brightly,
Echoing the call to wander
Along a path unknown,
Guiding gently by their sparkle.

Birds of the trees,
Beasts of the forest,
Unique utterings
Of their life's song.

What is your life's song?
It is unique.
From whence does it come?
To whom does it go?

Getting to Know ....!

We sat in a little oratory. Some people would not call it that. You see it is a front room in an ordinary country house. The setting is rural and beautifully pastoral; fields bedecked with the innocent lambs. The only breakthrough in the deep silence is the rushing roar of the speeding traffic along the A 40. The latter is the main artery to the coast, and on a summer's day it is beckoning its passengers and travellers along.

The house could be described as a two up and two down, except that there is an extension built on at the back on the ground floor. So, for the sake of the Council Tax, without which, nobody can exist, or have the right to exist, the extension adds a valuable contribution to the Tax Revenue. That is the fount of money so many people contribute to, to keep the play of politics on the road!

This is a noble cause, or could be, if properly used to lessen the dividing line separating the wealthy and the not so wealthy of the land. But it is part of the age-old story going back thousands of years; remember Matthew the tax collector and his "donations". They provoked a lot of adverse feelings. They are rooted in the history and folklore of civilisation.

The Master Himself was not oblivious of it; was He oblivious of anything? I can categorically say "No" to that question. He had some words of wisdom though, to enlighten our response. We could be proactive or reactive. Strangely His words, perhaps not heard by so many today, have a special ring about them. They echo at times through the deafness of our ears, like the dustbin lid. The warning is clear "Render to Caesar the things that are Caesar's ------ "Matt 22. I leave you to finish the quote.

As we sit and listen to the drowning noise of the engines, my attention is drawn to the sign outside the house. Oh the house, well in years past it would possibly have been the gatehouse to the mansion up the avenue and the farm beyond that again. Each of these has a life of its own now. In time, if not at present, they will be part of the anonymous "www." link!

The sign outside the house gives no indication of its dwellers. It is rather hard to miss this sign, though many very accomplished drivers passing by fail to take the message in, or see it. It is not within their ken thinking as they journey onwards! The sign is bold and clear, in truth it can't be missed, but can very easily be gracefully ignored. It reads, in the middle of a strong red sign, 40 in black. The guardians of the road, "Where are they?" you ask.

Well there is a well-hidden lay-by on the curve of the road, which is activated by a white car with blue stripes and as usual its occupants, in true style, wear caps! Their appearance is electrifying; the noise of the traffic diminishes as their driver's hands take control and the easing of pressure on the pedals renders a scene of not just law-abiding drivers but the most responsible citizens!

After about two hours of guardianship and the task a fait accompli, the white car with the blue stripes puts on its bleep and hits the dust of the road as it too speeds along. What complex creatures

71

inhabit this earth. I wonder are they the same everywhere!

The house stays standing. Its peaceful little garden stream flowing down the hill is in sharp contrast. It flows quietly and calmly on its course. There is no sign to halt it but nature itself has its own way of securing a safe passage. It certainly has a wisdom all of its own. Let me tell you it's secret.

It winds and winds, and as it reaches this catastrophic road, it just calmly ignores the blockage the road presents. Instead it winds its way and, with an air of "I am Ok", passes under the bridge to the open wide fields that greet it at the other side. So often this pawn of nature is so silent one wonders if it is still there.

From time to time the birds come and splash in the stream; ducks frequently take their sail along it from the other side for the afternoon. Then having had their picnic along the bank, they return home to their rightful owners. It is obvious to the onlooker that the silence of the stream, like the house, has a mission of its own which mankind so far, has not thought of interpreting.

Above all, what is most worthy of note is that the power the stream possesses does not weaken in the face of the storm. It, throughout time, has said to the gale force winds, "Enough is Enough, No Flooding on My Banks, please." And the winds obey!

A GLOW OF LIGHT

- As you surf the web of your inner life how do you resonate with the thrust of this story?
- Describe the landscape of your Dwelling Place through a medium of your choice i.e. word, art etc.
- Allow it to speak to you.

Scripture Reference: Matt 8, 23-27

Be still and ponder: Fear not, it is I.

How Could it Happen?

A young boy walked down a lane on a cold winter's afternoon. He was well wrapped up in his duffle coat and boots with a cap on his head. Who would have wondered where he was going?

There was really only one way for him, that is, if he kept to the road. He sauntered along, stopping now and then to look into the hedge. It was a road he travelled daily. This morning's trot was not so leisurely; he was on his way to school. The neighbours called it "Tudor Road" school. To him it was --- well he had his own name for it. Perhaps it is best not put into writing! It was not a place he hastened to with glee any morning, not least today! His heart was not animated by the thought of entering the assembly hall. It put a cold shudder up his spine.

He often spoke of this at home but nobody seemed to understand. "It was just his sensitive nature that felt pain when none was meant or inflicted," they said. That's what they thought. Today as he strode home after school his gait was a little lighter. He had his own plan of action. He could cope with the sarcastic remarks made by some pupils. He would ignore them, or could he?

He passed a gap in the hedge. Actually it was an old gate, one of those gates long since out of use. This was no obstacle to him. He heard a voice within him call out "Go for it Jack" and he decided to go! Had he not left the road already, now he would wind his way across the fields in the opposite direction.

Jack began to bounce along the side and over the ditches. The cows went on chewing the cud and the sheep rested under the trees. The scene they depicted contrasted sharply with what he felt within. There was no resting-place for him; there hadn't been for three years now. Why? Well he could not make that out either. He did no wrong to others but somehow they disliked him. Nothing pleased them. He strolled along. This time however he had a purpose in mind. He would make for the big city. He had seen it on the screen and read about it. The lure of the big lights and the shelter of a place where nobody knew him urged him on. It was a case of "far away hills are green!"

Yes, he had made preparations. Yesterday he had withdrawn some of his savings from the post office with the intention of replacing it at a future date. No, he was not going for good, just enough time to find himself and feel himself as a person who was not hounded by others.

He thought briefly about his parents and how they would feel. This became so strong a drawback to him that he let go of it and blanked it out of his mind. Easier not to think, not just now anyway!

As the evening closed in on him so did his isolation. He however was not afraid of the dark. He had some provisions in his bag, slung over his shoulder. It was time he thought to make the load lighter and dispose of some of the books in the ditches. His name had already been blanked out of them. He didn't consider how modern technology would scan these books when they were found and reveal his secret. Then mission accomplished, he went on his journey.

As luck would have it, as he reached the main road the stars shone brightly and kindly upon him; he saw a truck approach. He watched it; it was slowing down. It stopped and he jumped in. He was on the high road to new life!

Three days later he is almost anaesthetised by the hunger and cold of going rough and trying to avoid even more hostile reactions from the passers-by. Would he try to return home, he thought! He definitely said "No", not till he had proved himself by his own skill to be in charge of his own life. Then with a distinctive air, he would return!

A lady passed by. Jack was huddled up outside a supermarket. The smell of fresh bread coming through the door filled his nostrils but not the hunger space within him. He longed for home, though he would not admit it. The lady stopped. She spoke kindly to him. Maybe she had a son of her own and understood. He replied to all her questions and even amazed himself at the story he spun her. He had an air of confidence now. She believed him and what he said mattered to her. This was like a fresh breeze on a dark, damp day of his life! Kindly she offered to get him some food so now he eagerly awaited her return.

She returned. Some "Good to Eat" foods come out of the bags: cheese sandwiches, apples, big yoghurt and a spoon, to name but a few things. He thanked her graciously and sadly looked at her as she left for home! A deep longing came upon him but he was made of sterner stuff than that, he mused.

What Jack had not realised was that that day a whole new life had opened up before him. He had broken with the past and taken control of his life, sadly. Many years later, sitting on London Bridge he wondered what had befallen his youthful hopes and ambitions. Alas, he felt there was no turning back or was there? Now Jack's history remains untold and the pangs of his heart went with him to the grave.

A GLOW OF LIGHT

- Young people are vulnerable and there is a child within each of us.
- How do you respond to the hurtful events of life?
- Can you identify them with your inner child's experience?

Unload your burden on to Yahweh,
And he will support you.   Psalm 55

Come to Me

Yes my arms entwine you,
Feel the touch.
What does it say to you?

Hear the silent message
Of the air around you.
Can you hear it?
Keep it close to your heart.

My arms are those of your God,
Yahweh who led his people
Generation after generation.
Today I start a new generation.

My little ones will come to me,
Entwined in your love of them.
Pain is theirs,
But so am I.

Listen to that pain.
See the new baby within them.
It will come to life,
My life.

A Spoonful of Sugar

I was tired that night in mid-October sitting by the fire. Its glow seemed to warm the whole house, not just the room; I sat there and relaxed. I gazed into the fire as we did as children so long ago. I remembered the good days of childhood so long past. The scene became alive to me. It was the days of the radio, no satellite or digital, no mobiles to interrupt the calm of the house.

I could clearly see, in my memory, my father sitting by the fire. That was his seat on the left. He had the poker in his hand as he gently moved the burning wood and coal to give out more heat. On a winter's night we often decided to make some toast on the burning coals. Our little hands would hold the toasting fork till we called for help! The heat would burn through, or so we thought, our gentle childlike skin.

We realised hands were not made for burning; they had a purpose of their own. It was then my father would take the fork and our longing eyes would watch the golden transformation of the bread. But oh, what a smell rose to the ceiling. It would cause a sharpened appetite to develop and demand more!

My mother, on call as usual, would produce the plates and butter, enhanced with homemade jam. That is right. It was made by her own loving hands and most notable of all, the children (that was us) were the first to be treated with it. One could see the joy in my mother's eyes as she watched our delight.

These were precious moments. For many years they were taken as normal! It was the only life we knew. The famous radio programs duly entertained us, as this faraway, invisible man spoke from behind the wooden structure, called the Radio. This had a place of honour in the sitting room and was usually turned on and off by the master of the house, my father.

Then there were the delightful times when we had our own circus, by the fire. It was then that my father would take on the role of magician. How we loved it as he spun china plates in a circle, with one hand, my mother holding her breath, lest one had a sudden "death" as it hit the floor! I can't ever remember it happening but I can vividly see the quickened heartbeat of my mother. She would declare "That is one of our wedding gifts!" Wedding gifts were the precious treasures, meant to last for life.

My life has gone on. The years have passed and somehow this richness remains with me forever. Tonight as I sit I am somewhat more bewildered by my awareness of how many of the human race, though living on the same planet, had not a childhood peace like mine.

Rather they experienced very troubled waters. Story after story, I have heard, of how the longing for normality had to be fed, by a blocking out of reality and an entering into fantasy-land to maintain a compos mentis to survive. These fantasies emerge in various forms and shapes of survival kits.

Have you ever touched on these survival kits? They are made of very different types of material.

Some seem like waterproof cloaks and boots. The problem with this type is they could let the water in and cause the wearer to sink. There are also the life jackets, so strong and hard to the touch, that they allow no other helping hand on their hearts. In a way, they are lucky to keep breathing! The list is endless; the long solitary walk, the sitting in isolation watching the fires of their lives go out. That is the danger zone as there is no dad with the poker to stir up the quenching flames and kindle them anew.

Have you ever watched the smouldering ashes come to life and blaze anew with a spoonful of sugar? Perhaps that is what these folks need I thought, as I contemplated the happy days of my young life. A life blessed by loving memories.

The spoonful of sugar is very important. It used to be rationed during the war days. Sugar together with the butter and oranges were off the shopping list by necessity. Life deprived of such luxuries was regarded as hard. I smile when I recall the day we heard that oranges, big Jaffa oranges, were back on the shelves of the shops! Normality was returning with their sweet and energising juice.

The old man next door was reminiscing the other day. With one hand on his stick and a smile on his face he declared, "Oh for a lump of sugar to sweeten my day." His eyes looked with longing. He too longed for the spoonful to pick him up. Perhaps it is the T.L.C. and the spoonful of sugar that we all need. This luxury, these days, is so often rationed and curtailed in our world of plenty!

A GLOW OF LIGHT

- What ingredients need to be nourished in your life to enkindle new life into some smouldering ashes?
- Does the thought of giving a "spoonful of sugar" grip you?
- Where is your vision leading you?

Open our hearts Lord to the movement of your Spirit on the strings of our hearts.

The Mouse

Her hand swept swiftly over the keys. Yes, it was the keys of the computer. This vast encyclopaedia of knowledge hailed by many as the greatest invention of the twentieth century.

The monitor came to life with the opening page of deep-sea frogs and myriads of underwater life being exposed on a twelve-inch screen. The fish, with their blue tails, frisked about in joyful glee unaware that they too were caught up in the worldwide net of computerisation. They presented an aquarium dimension to the rhythm of the gurgling sound superimposed by the modern mind of computer experts. It was intriguing to behold. But where to from here for the fish? Well the fish had no say in this matter. They were with a gentle touch of the mouse to be relegated to the depths of oblivion, at least for the present.

The mouse, it had its rightful place in this organisation. It was very important. Actually it was a V.I.P. for without it the whole orbit of this seemingly unsophisticated box, 18 inches wide, would have no purpose. I say the mouse, for that is what they named it in the lengthy list of instructions, which accompanied the box.

It got its name from the shape of its body which gently fits under the palm of one's hand and also, the most indicative of all reasons, it's long winding tail. This mouse, not created as part of the animal world, had a mighty long tail, which as it moved swiftly and silently, let the world know that it had a power of its own. In fact it controlled the machine! The experts had to obey its orders and commands. A quick click to the right when it should have been to the left or vice versa could cause havoc. It just did not like being played about with by amateurs. Remember I said it had a very definite V.I.P. status! Just like all V.I.Ps of this world, whatever the occasion, the red carpet was expected to be rolled out for them.

Well this mouse had no ordinary carpet under its feet. It had a static one called, rather unbecomingly, a mat. The mouse didn't seem to mind that, though human VIPs would feel utterly rejected, if given such a "high" profile. This mouse, as I indicated, is no ordinary mouse, so its mind works on a different set of values. It is fully aware that the Red Carpet Brigade will never be out on display like him as he walks across the screen, but who minds that! The mouse is so important that it sits like a monarch and controller of all it surveys on a specially woven mat. This mat portrays many aspects of life, from scenes to rainbows; from movies to company advertising and of course the images of pet dogs or even a fox!

The value of this mat is inestimable as it sits on the desk, the reliable footstool and foundation base of the irreplaceable mouse. Together they send out a world message, "We, though small, are of the utmost importance." The caption on their flag heralds the inestimable value of this creature. In large red print the writing reads "The Importance of Being Small"!

That mouse is a cute little creature of man's invention. As I said, in this little body and long tail, it has the power to control all manipulation of the machine. 'All' means the massive worldwide electronic encyclopaedia. How astonishing a feat!

One sample of this control freak, or so it may be thought to be, is that if it so wishes it can sit and refuse to work. You can go click, click for as long as you like, but it holds the reins and even more astonishing, can leave its perplexed owner staring at a crashed screen! Even this marvellous invention of the 20th century can be left like a disused, faceless complex in the face of this little mouse. One wonders how it, the mouse, feels at being so important, so powerful in these moments of its history. What is it really trying to say to us, the masters of civilisation?

I sense that, deep within it, is a little voice, with a rare sense of humour, which silently broadcasts its message of the power and glory of the humble and the often unrecognised power of little creatures on this earth.

A GLOW OF LIGHT

- Which component of the computer do you identify with and how?
- What flagship do you fly?
- Would you wish to change your image?

Scripture Reference: Micah 6,8.

> This is what Yahweh asks of you,
> Only this, to act justly,
> To love tenderly,
> And walk humbly with your God.

Is There a Timetable?

The train jogged its way along the single line railway. Its sound was melodious and captivated the imagination. You may be surprised that I say "melodious" because there are many other sounds that would merit the title, or for that matter, relate to a train – The Fantasia of Schubert's Swan Lake to name but one! In my mind as I write I can hear Schubert's Trout peacefully infiltrating my consciousness with its call to a deep relaxation of my inner being.

I say melodious song of the train and that is what it is compared to the noise that dinned my ears for the past hour and a half on this five hour journey. It is holiday time on board this train and so its occupants ranging from two months to eighty odd years and octogenarian plus, have taken their place in this one long carriage train. Their destinations vary. There was great relief at the last stop. The picturesque town of Builth Wells had called them to itself. This week the origins of its history and a rolling back of time has reincarnated itself in the town. What is so fascinating about Victorian days, one wonders?

Meanwhile the quietness of the train's occupants hung over us like a canopy on a sunny day, which had been designed to shelter its occupants from the burning heat, while at the same time affording a pleasant view of Brecon Beacons as it winds along its valleys. This is music to the eye of the beholder as well as to the ear!

I sit back and ponder the wonder of the mountains, created by the invisible hand of the Maker in His great work of creation. These mountains were no "quick fix"- definitely not. Once a little boy asked his teacher "Why did God take seven days to make the world"? She appeared perplexed and then unconvincingly narrated, step by step, the approach of God the Mastermind, to an even more perplexed child! Maybe the sheep on the hills today could, in their own language, make a more enlightened statement. Who knows! You see I came to that conclusion without any rational proof or scientific research. The mind boggles; would it not have been interesting if I had stumbled on a source of knowledge! The cutting edge is that nobody has ever yet spoken to the sheep throughout the centuries, and recorded their reply. It would be interesting too, to ask the age-old shepherds, who allowed the sheep and goats to graze together, what they thought. But to them, silence is golden!

Those words re-echo for me a feeling of immense rays of sunshine flooding over our beings. Are they really felt? Are they allowed to penetrate and, like the prism, in due time radiate shafts of penetrating light and enlightenment? I stop to think this out, and it seems as if I have unearthed a huge Pandora box for myself and taken its lid off! The secrets within are as untold as those of the Master's mind when creation was created. I invite you, the reader, to enter into the wonder of the Pandora box presenting itself to you in those silent moments of penetrating light.

Yes the train is on its course. It is climbing or trying to climb Brecon Beacons, in the hope of reaching the other side and a straight path. God only knows if it will! As I gaze over the hills I see a path winding around the summit, two thirds of the way up.

From where I sit it looks like a simple walking path that affords an easy way for the energetic and enthusiastic walker, and climber, who has made it that far. A thought has just struck me – I wonder what the climbers had to eat today before setting out, to fortify their being against the pangs of hunger? What is in that knapsack over their shoulders? Water to refresh their parched systems perhaps and a pack to nibble at! On second thoughts, is that knapsack only a facade for the invisible hiking sheet and the empty bottle that they are really carrying?

Then I wonder why the pathway, throughout time, has been walked into the mountain at that angle and circumscribing it! Why didn't the climber go straight to the top? Obviously that would have been a shorter walk. Is it the lure or the trick of the mountain that led them that way? Maybe it is the height of it that puts off the inevitable last moments of the climb. Those mountains know our way of thinking – that process of the mind that tells us 'tomorrow will do'. Like St. Augustine we pray, 'not today Lord, later!' Eventually we will climb the eternal mountain one day, having gone round it by various routes.

Sometimes too, like the perplexed mind of a child, we can journey on arriving at no conclusion. Meanwhile The Master sits and silently awaits our "now", like the old lady who looks out and, through her open door, awaits a visitor. Time does not seem to rush on when one is climbing the mountain. It never did. The evolution of the world has taken billions of years of The Master's time but what a creation He blessed us with!

A GLOW OF LIGHT

- How does the lure of the mountain impact on you, the hiker?
- I invite you the reader, to enter into this wonder of the Pandora Box presenting itself to you in those silent moments of penetrating light.
- What provisions have you made for the journey?

Who shall climb the mountain of the Lord? Psalms 24.

Lord of the Mountains

Lord of the Mountains
You speak no words.
Silence – your utterings,
Calm cool water
Within my Being
Springing forth in fountains
Fountains of love,
Yet, unforeseen.

Immense your Presence
Powerful, unacknowledged so often
Deep balm for the heart that seeks you.

Call forth our Being
Wrap it in awareness,
Awareness of the Presence within.
Cause us to stop, gaze and wonder
At the guest we hold within.

We are your Mountains, Lord.
Your Presence speaks from within us.
Presence of Wonder, Awe
And Amazement
At the mercy that flows from within.

Mountains calling forth
Faith in response.
Faith beholding
Every touch of our creation.

Oh, gift of Hope,
Do we dare to hope?
The finished masterpiece
Will reflect your Majesty?

It is Called Progress

It was Thursday, midday, and I had ambled my way into a city church. The church was situated amid the uprooting of the past, which held the history of the city in its hands. For many years now there was talk of renovating and modernising the infamous and famous city centre, called the Bull Ring. Anyone who knew the city knew the Bull Ring! It was the landmark - what the Leaning Tower of Pisa is to France. It had been opened many years ago, announcing the invasion of modernisation and hailed as one great piece of architecture, surrounded by myriads of underground passages around the city. It, too, looked down on the city from its ivory tower.

The latter however conveyed the image of a thirteen-storey glasshouse, with its engraved importance, visible to all who dared to look that high in the face of oncoming traffic. The sign read 'Birmingham Bullring'. You can guess the origins of its name and wonder as you gaze at storey after storey of glass in the shape of a ring. At its feet, as I said, lay rings of traffic called roundabouts, with safety zones for pedestrians. This was the proposed idea and longed-for wish of the architects.

Today it is experiencing a new era of its presence - total demolition of all the underground passes and roundabouts. They have had their day. This is the new era of State of the Art, as they call it! Which art, one is never sure as they wind their way round the developing creation of manpower or is it womanpower? Today the paths to be trod, the lights to be pressed and greeted by the green man, inevitably have moved or ceased to function.

The mind boggles as the streams of traffic, buses and cars learn new points of direction. Yesterday there was no entrance to the high street. Today it's one-way traffic but diverts suddenly, to the amazement of all, in the opposite direction. One can only conclude that the mighty architects of movement and control do not risk their own lives in this city behind a wheel, at least till normality appears on the horizon, whatever that might be! The old market place has had a new body given to it and, stage-by-stage, celebrities opened its doors to the awe-struck shoppers and the disappointment of many who had hoped to keep the status quo and all its cultural traditions.

Now the minds of the people are being prepared for the so- called Grand Opening in two weeks' time. Oh yes it will be a Grand Opening, that is after the rush and exasperation of those who have laboured to create the instructions computerised in some unknown machine. It will be a day for off with the yellow helmets and boots and on with the tops and distinguished guests. The chains of office will hang around the mayor's neck like a polished up jewel from the Tower! There will be speeches congratulating the names on the big display posters which announced the arrival of the new city. No, it is not nominated as Cultural City of Europe, but that is another story wrapped up in its history.

It is not a cultural city by virtue of its buildings and grandeur but by the very presence of its people. The face of creation, in a true sense, gives life to the city by its multiracial composition - an aspect of richness that perhaps is not as applauded as the buildings. I cannot resist asking the question – which dimension, buildings or people, are in truth the wealth of the city, if properly cared for?

Yes, the people will have their place at the Grand Opening. Mass-media coverage would be of no avail without them. Last night the News Reader, preparing the minds of people for the great feast of history, invited those who wished to attend to contact them. She said they would have a very important role awaiting them, namely "To clap their hands with as much noise as a dustbin lid would make." Is this their privilege, I wondered, to proclaim the great and mighty who appear on stage?

I did not mention the church: it appears to have got a share of the booty in the massive pedestrian barriers erected outside its doors. There is a little space to pass through to get in to the door. Quite considerate of the authorities I should think! It is somewhat like saying, "It would be easier to pass through the eye of an needle." What effect has this on the presence of the church in this costly modernisation? Oh, it also got a new ramp for people with disability. I looked and pondered what are the priorities, equality or inequality? I forgot to mention that another church, deep in the middle of this wonderland, hailing in the 21st.century, had its golden cock re-erected with shimmering glee. A case in point one might say!

Ah, the church with the barrier, well it is a humble dwelling built in a back street, hard to find unless you know the direction of a famous store and then wind your way. It, I mean the church, has its own history. It was built at a time when they, that breed of churches like its people, had to be hidden. No, it was not acceptable to "society life." But from its humble origins it has developed a presence of service to the humble shopper and often the gentleman or woman, that shelter from the cold in its back benches. They know a real presence in this back street little home. That presence, which no architect could humanly build, is the presence of the very Master of architects in known history!

A GLOW OF LIGHT

- Have you experienced any phases of restoration in your life's history?
- How up building were they and why?
- How important is the role of God's people in creating a just society reflecting his love of all, irrespective of class or creed?

If Yahweh does not build the house,
In vain the masons toil.   Psalm 127

Garden - Open for Viewing

The garden lay open before us, like one mighty picturesque book, page by page, revealing the treasure within. This book was not made of paper, even parchment paper, nor was it hand painted in the most delicate of colours and illustrated by careful sketches of a pen or pencil. There were no watercolours here either. Rather it was a rich tapestry of unbelievable beauty.

People walked along and through its winding paths. It was part of a relaxing afternoon trip out into the open countryside. Actually, some of the visitors were on a mystery tour! They had no idea how this garden came into their orbit or why the tour operator took them there. It was for them just one of those stops en route. The highlight of course was the riverside café and the cream teas, a treat for the weary soul!

To others it was a place they had thought of visiting when a suitable day presented itself to them, and above all, when they would have time to walk amid the splendour of the spring tapestry. A vast range of colour penetrated their eyes, colours and variety they would never have mingled together. All seemed so much in harmony to the naked eye of the one who gazed on them. Yes they would take some lessons from this trip, even the frail daffodils blowing in the wind were an infusion of thought into their hearts. How lovely it would be to plant, no not this year it is too late, some of these bulbs in their front garden they thought. What a display it would make!

One lady, very much into gardening, consulted her husband, a retired businessman. His response was not very enthusiastic, the gardening bug had not hit him yet! She on the other hand gloatingly talked of the wonderful display with which they could adorn their home. It could be unique: well there was no chance of irrigating a river or stream through it but "Why not a fountain?" she asked. The idea grew more elaborate as her imagination moved into gear. It was possibly in fourth gear and ready to go into autopilot! "Can you see the reaction on the neighbours' faces?" she inquired, not so jokingly, for now she was entering the plains of reality, if only in her thoughts. Oh yes, this could set a new trend in gardening. He, the husband, who was more inclined to whack up the lawn as he enthusiastically practiced his golf, became more silent if not switched off. Perhaps he was envisaging this new garden trend of fountains! At last he spoke, " What a catastrophe if every garden in the cul-de-sac had a fountain." I listened as I overheard the conversation and became convinced that, perhaps, they themselves were in a cul-de-sac! What a response, I thought, to the creative picture of colour and beauty.

I moved along not wishing to be considered eavesdropping. To my amazement I sat under a laburnum tree on a seat carved from a tree trunk. The very touch of the wood itself was a wonder. I was touching nature over which humans have no power except to destroy. What a fearful thought! People could not cause it to come into being, only destroy it. I pondered the vast areas of forestry in the world, cut down for paper. I was then distracted as I saw before my mind's eye the headlines printed on some of this paper. What a desecration of one the wonders of creation, as well as the lives of the people it portrayed or sought to influence.

There was a brighter side to my thoughts also. I walked through the neatly trimmed lawns with the mount at the end to be climbed, even by the elderly for it was not steep. It featured a footpath that wound round and gently took one to the top. There the mind of the planter had carefully and picturesquely planted the elms. There were twelve of them to remind us of the apostles, and a centre one, with its own raised "platform" of honour for the master Himself. The walk was like a little pilgrimage in time into a deep ocean, hiding its secret in the depths of my being. What was it doing to me? Unearthing something I suppose deep in my nature that needed to stand like the elms in the presence of its Maker. Could that be left like the visit to the garden for another day? I guess not.

As I left the garden I remembered hearing on the radio about these trees. No, it was not about their beauty, but their shavings. These, in due time each year, are carefully trimmed off by the head gardener. This caused more growth for the next year. The wonderful point about them however is that the shavings, having fallen to the ground, are gathered carefully and recycled for medical relief purposes. What a wonderful purpose in life these shavings fulfilled! I was silenced into thinking, what of my own shavings?

A GLOW OF LIGHT

- How do you nurture the garden of beauty within you?
- How open is it to receive the "visits" of nature in season?
- How precious and life giving are your shavings?

Scripture Reference:

Unless the grain of wheat falls to the ground and dies,
it remains but a grain.   John 12:24

Beginnings and Endings

I awoke this morning to hear the birds chirping their rising song to each other. I have heard this song many times before, but this morning it seemed different. Yes, as I became conscious after a very restful night, I realised it was my birthday. For some days now I had been looking forward to it, and I wondered why this time!

The bones did not seem any stiffer and the compos mentis could be rated as normal (that is given the age!) I greeted this new year of my life with joy for the past. Did I ever think I would reach this landmark! Then I thought, "Isn't every birthday, and for that matter every moment, a land-mark not just in my history?"

What is the surprise of today, I wondered expecting none. Was there somewhere lurking a seed of new hope? The hours passed leisurely at first; then it happened. I was taken over by Dyson! A neighbour had offered me a trial of her new Dyson. Now I was hitting the top rank of the commercial world.

Its bright trimmings smiled at me and the green knob on the right invited me to press it. Yes, but only for a moment. I now had all the power in the world behind me to rejuvenate my carpets. That is truly a fancy name for what graces my floors, but they suffice.

Slowly I moved this power into action as I said, but even it had to face some obstacles on its path. Oh they were only the ordinary simple things that exist, and sometimes even function, in a room. The chairs seemed to cringe as this new monster approached them. Then there was the bookstand and the table, for starters! I turned off the power as I realised that even this monster could not function without a continual injection of power from a hidden source in the face of obstacles.

The white box on the wall appeared so tiny and insignificant in comparison to "Mr. Dyson." No one can see the power of this tiny white object but, switched on, it invigorates and causes the combustion to roar. Then any object however insignificant and unwanted, like dust and threads, becomes a victim of its power of suction. The more I thought about the reality of this the more interesting it became for me!

You see I saw dust lingering around the carpets quite happily, up to now. Nobody had put it there, no eye had seen it descend or breathe like a human being. Who called it dust and why? Oh, the threads were easy to see and the little bits that had dropped, no not of their own freewill. Accidentally is a polite way of stating the case.

They had been dropped by one of the inhabitants of its planet and space. I say space because each carpet has its own special room and rightful place in this house. From day one they had made their presence felt here.

They were indeed very much appreciated, and they in turn afforded a soft, comforting feeling for its inhabitants. It is true the inhabitants walked on them, spilt tea on them or, even worse, wine or coffee in their less appreciating moments. Yes, they had their air of ownership over the carpets that touched their feet with warmth!

I tried to enter the mind of the carpet. It had from infancy to old age been subjected to the appreciation of other people. Once it appeared off the loom all eyes were on it. They felt the texture and assessed its colour and pattern. Its qualities of endurance and tolerance were also brought into question.

To some it passed the test; others thought that to opt to choose it was too high a price. It must have been a strange start to what one calls life! That word, I mean "life" was also bandied about. They, the on-lookers or prospective buyers, also questioned its durability.

Obviously the poor old carpet had a rough start in life. Its very existence as a profit making presence was brought into question. At times it could even denote in the voice of the buyer a note of rejection. Yet it hung on that stand and no word was uttered by it!

It, like the big Dyson, had no power of its own to speak or walk or even to make a stand to display its case. Somehow, even in these early days, it knew its fate.

It would someday fulfil its role as a carpet and finally be rejected, once again, by a mere human and sent to a scrap heap. Its fate in life was already a certainty. Like Dyson, its days could soon be numbered!

A GLOW OF LIGHT

- The tapestry of life takes on many different and various hues.
- How would you give artistic expression to yours?
- How do you view the tapestry of other people's lives?

Scripture Reference:

You are precious in my eyes.   Jeremiah 1: 5

Mystery of all Mysteries

"My soul is sorrowful even onto death." These words, spoken out of great love over two thousand years ago, came to my mind today. They are power-filled words, with so many stories within them. Yes, the storyteller of all times summed up his life with them, though they were not his last words.

They ring of pain, deep pain, a pain that can only be understood by those who, in some little way, are in touch with the pain of their own burden. Here was a man fully conscious of not physical pain, but a pain that longed for perhaps someone to realise his pain. His was a pain of longing, longing to heal the human race.

Like the person who longs for physical healing or emotional healing, he was making a statement, the cry of which can never be stopped. His words however are full of hope. The reader gets the message – "In death it will end in triumph."

I watched a documentary one night, on children and adults who have suffered brain damage in various degrees and ways. A number are being medically traced back to birth. Somehow the flow of oxygen was not permeating the brain. In many cases it remained a mystery. I have known people who have witnessed and lived with this happening to their child. As I go down memory lane I am faced with the dilemma, the dilemma of not being able to unravel the mystery of "Why?" One tends to put it into the "box" and close up one's thinking power. I ask, "Is it because it is too painful or I feel wanting?"

A mother's softly spoken words came to mind, " I do not know how I can go on." This re-echoes the great Master of pain as he spoke his words. He too was human and in some mysterious way I hear him answering her. She goes on. Her world is an unknown world to many.

As I, quite in a comfortable position, ponder this woman I am like the postman going from door to door with his cargo of mail. Have you ever observed him? He checks the resident's number and the mouth of the door opens its jaws and devours the contents, with no due respect for the matter contained or the feelings of the recipients. There is no voice at the receiving end. Who knows if they are there or even dead or alive! The postman has done his rounds; all is well. But is it?

This woman's cry re-echoes in my ears. Have I just received her plea in words, digested it and left her uncared for at the receiving end of my presence? The media tell us all is well; old and young are being cared for. How I wonder? Like the child who stands and gazes at his bike with its stabilizers, I hesitate to get on this bike and peddle my way along the road of empathy with her. No she is not looking for sympathy, just empathy, for me to give a pain relieving touch to her heartbreak. The heartbreak, which is hidden deep down beneath the smile, which states, "All is well with me!"

I sit by the sea. The ideas, and lack of them, come and go like the ebbing sea on the shore, leaving behind a hint of their presence. I have read about children too, and have known them; some of them, in a way too painful for me to really stop and think about. Is it because I feel so helpless in the face of their existence?

Research shows that they too while proclaiming so much affection and love to their nearest and dearest, at times can also experience deep within a very heart-breaking cry, a cry that could be re–echoing that of the Lord himself. Their utter confusion, anxiety and fear in the face of unknown objects, people or situations is immeasurable. Somewhere deep within them is a cry that they feel unable to express or even make sense of. They as I sit, speak so vibrantly to me of His presence among us. Today I am drawn to enter their world. They are his gift to us. I feel so helpless in their almighty presence, a presence that portrays to a somewhat blind audience, His great strength of being able to live on, while crying aloud with a cocktail of joy and mesmerisation. Like the sun, they too can melt our hearts.

A GLOW OF LIGHT

- How do you try to explain the mystery of pain?
- Sit in silence with His words.

Scripture reference: Matt. 26:38

My soul is sorrowful to the point of death.

An Invitation

Behold my Mother,
A woman frail to behold,
The loss of a son she adored,
Now stands silent
Beneath the beam of Love.

Cast your eyes upon Him.
Let her stillness speak my love,
Love without words,
Love of a gaze.

Now come, take your place
Beside her.
Silently stand and
Allow me to speak.

The Secret of the Author

It was a dark night, the kind of night that entices one to sit by the fire and relax with a book, a good book. I say "good", you know the choice. It takes you through its endless pages, and small print, on a fascinating journey into make believe land. It's a "Who done it?" Right, that is the one that sets the adrenaline flowing and the words pop from the pages. Your intellect jets into speed and the guessing game starts and accelerates. Yes, you the reader are in control as you eye each word with hastening breath.

It was this kind of night for Muriel. She had bought it in a shop, a charity shop, today. Her idea was to keep it for a wet night. 'Wet', that word could have many meanings, not just tone of climate. Well tonight was wet. She was aware of the weather but also felt she would like a trip down a new avenue of her mind and so she stepped out en route! As the time passed she was getting enthralled yes, but also agitated. She, it appears, was not really getting on the mystery of this story. It seemed so real, yet each time she came up with the possible "doer", she was led another step on by the writer or was it her imagination?

"How frustrating", she mused to herself. I really thought I knew where the story was leading me. It is playing a game of cat and mouse with me and the only fact that I am fully aware of is that I cannot leave the book down! To do so would in my opinion be defeatism. That was certainly a word that she could not allow to be imprinted on her vocabulary list. She would go on. Sometime the mystery would be seen to the naked eye in word.

Oh, she would go right on now although it was time to relax. Relax! I thought that was what she was doing up to now! With the power of her intellect and the gift of sight she was seeing and hearing a mystery unfold. Captivating perhaps, but it could also be a mighty escape route from resting, or resisting the impact of what was really on her mind: a little of both, one could presume.

The thought of a cup of tea and a chocolate biscuit was enticing. That would revive the drooping spirit within her. Soon the kettle proclaimed it had reached its boiling point. Moments later Muriel was ensconced in her armchair. Who would wish for more! It was one of those most enticing chairs. With a switch of a button one was fully stretched out and Muriel, with her headrest and feet up, was queen in her own palace!

She eagerly returned to page 91 and hastily decided the gardener had done it. The plot was now unfolding more clearly for her. "Why did I not see this before", she thought. Ho! that is me. I jump on the wagon of thought process and most times become a non-starter. It is like the crossword, she thought and smiled to herself. It is good for the mind, they say. It keeps the old brain box machine ticking over. It sharpens it up too.

Muriel knew this for she was an addict of the boxes and clues. Full speed ahead was her tactic and it seemed to work, that is, till another clue presented itself in bold print. It seemed to roar, "No, you will not beat me. I have the secret of this puzzle, not you!"

On these occasions she would put down the crossword with some reluctance. Maybe her reaction indicated why it was called crossword! With a sense of hidden defeat, no she would not admit it, the crossword was put aside, aside but not for good. Tomorrow was another day. First things first, as the papers arrived, she would enlighten her mind with the real and true solution. "Why did I not think of that?" she would mutter to herself, as once again the lesson of returning to the source of the object portrayed itself.

Well tonight it was the mystery story. Fully convinced it was the gardener, she fingered the pages with glee, only to be confused again when he appeared to slip the net. She, the reader or recipient, was gradually losing the plot. Losing it more and more, stage by stage to the source of this mystery - the writer himself!

By now she was less enthusiastic but more curious to know where the plot was going. She was tempted to turn to the last page to unravel the mystery of 'who and how'. The temptation was strong but would the last page really reveal it? She wondered, "Why do I become so involved!" It is only a story, or is it only a story?

Then she sat and reminisced about all the stories she had read and heard during her life, even the schoolgirls' magazine versions. They all had a way forward, a point which caused one to think anew. In a strange and silent way too, they were stored in the memo box of the individual and were part of this innate thinking and consequently influenced their lives.

What was striking now was that their writers, called authors, were unknown to them. Oh yes, they knew a little about them. They had read about them in the past. This was impacting on her mind tonight. She would have to sift through each word of the mystery, convinced she would find the "Who done it?"

It appeared to her a little uncomfortable position to be in. Anxiety to come to grips, find the clues and even perhaps feel she was ahead of the author was rising up like clouds on the horizon. How strange, she thought, that the very existence of the words, their plot and the readers they would touch, were quite definitely in the power of the writer and originator of the plot. Like all mysteries of life, we humans fail to penetrate them. The reason is, that that is what we are - mysteries owned by their creator!

A GLOW OF LIGHT

- How akin are you to Muriel in trying to unravel the Mystery of life?
- What emotions does this inability evoke in you?
- Be still and ponder:

Scripture reference: John 6, 67-68

"To whom shall we go, you have the message of eternal life."

Touched by the Light of Memory

A young man named Jack was kicking a ball, with great delight, towards his young son. Aged two years old, Jason was the apple of his eye. He could see himself in him and possibly, if he were open enough to himself, see his own dream. Yes he had a dream now that this bundle of joy would grow up, have a family and a loving young wife.

That seems like an everyday event, but as he kicked the ball and bounced off his foot, it touched something deep within him. "What is happening to me," he thought. "What am I feeling, something strange!" He tried to ward off thinking about it. It is no use now delving into what might have been, or so he thought.

The roar of laughter from his son brought him to consciousness again. You see Jason had actually saved a goal. Actually two coats made up the goal posts, having been carefully placed there by his father! The thrill and delight was sharp to the ear. Who could fail to hear it or for that matter resist taking note of it? Jack was amused, his son was obviously learning fast. Perhaps someday he would become a professional. This would relive Jack's lost dream!

"What matters?" he thought, "This is where I am in my life now". Still the pangs of unease stirred in his mind. Why was all this coming up now, at a time when he felt some sense of fulfilment? The game went on, he kicked the ball and watched the little feet aim to copy him and return it with glee.

How simple life seems to be through the eyes of a child! Looking back it is not how he would have described his own. It was rather the opposite. It was indeed like a cliff-hanger, so many times he had to hang in there. No, it was not a simple experience but a harrowing one. So often he could not put words on it or make sense of it. Everyone seemed against him, or were they? I mean his father.

The mother lay silent and one could be forgiven for thinking she was dormant or sleeping through their life's span. "Maybe it was all she could do", he thought. One way of coping was to blank out life. Yes, he needed to do this with greater determination. Nothing must prevent him from enjoying the fullness of life now. His Jason was everything to him!

I say everything. His mother Megan had long since, well it seemed like that, departed their lives. She journeyed on her life; her life and theirs had parted. Jason to some extent, if not entirely, was unaware of this. Where was she? Jack had no idea, though he felt he still loved her. What if she saw Jason now? Would the tide of time be turned back? There was little hope of that he thought. Fate is not as kind as that! They continued to play. Jack was a little more distracted now for his mind was ticking over faster.

At that moment he looked again, this time not at the ball but at Jason. He was flat out on the ground. What a shock! He gasped and hurled himself down on the grass, only to grasp his tiny beloved son in his arms. Jason was still; no sound or murmur from him. In a flash of thought he remembered his first aid. Yes it was a long time since he had done first aid – and he never practiced it. Now was the definite moment.

He set to. He opened the little neck of the shirt to let the air flow, the breath of life from him to this innocent little child, so innocent, and yet in the eyes of the world, disadvantaged. He had no mother to cuddle him, alas. Jack went through the motions of trying to resuscitate his son, his greatest joy. Silently his heart giving of its own breath tried to give life or sustain it. He clung in there nothing would stop him. This was his son.

A moment of calm and the little muscles of Jason's heart seemed to take on life! Somebody had noticed and the sound of the ambulance rang like music in his ears. Help, yes help was with him. He gained more strength as his hope increased. The gentle but strong hands of the medical team took over. Jack went silent. He could only stand by now and hope. Yes, he remembered his own mother always called on God in time of need.

This was such a time. He had not needed this before but now he did. The words sprang up deep within his longing heart. Help, Help! At that moment Jason was lifted into the ambulance and the blue flashing lights resounded down the road. He held his hands. Never had a touch been so deep and meaningful. They arrived in time.

After a lapse of time, it seemed like days, the doctor approached through a door. "You can go in now," he said, "Your little son will live." The emotions pent up over this time, and long before it, erupted. The joy of life had released a well of tears and anguish, so long suppressed. He felt silly. Men do not cry. "Stop it", he said to himself but the very depths of his being were out of control now. Some invisible hand had pulled the plug out and the tide of emotions was surging high. In a quiet secluded corner of the hospital he came to himself again. This time a deep peace filled his being. What had happened? Oh yes, he had Jason back in his life, but things had changed – he had!

He gathered himself and the kind nurse took him to see Jason. The little angelic face shone up at him, completely unaware of the great impact he had on his father's life. Jack stood over the bed. Words would have been an intrusion into their mutual loving affection. In a very peculiar way the heart-breaking moments, they felt like years, had changed his life. This is like a miracle he thought. The past is past. My wife, loved by me, I will give her freedom. In that act of his will Jack found his own true freedom, a freedom born out of intense pain and a longing to give his own life for his son.

A GLOW OF LIGHT

- What moments of Light changed you as a person and how?
- Silently ponder.

Scripture reference: Isaiah 9, 1

The people who walk in darkness have seen a great light.

Move Towards the Sun

The train, a high speed one, passed my window this afternoon. It was said to be "the" high speed of all time. Its glory would be the supreme task of conveying its precious body of people at one hundred and sixty miles per hour, or is it kilometers? No, I do not think the engineers had done a transition, mentally I mean, from miles to kilometers. Having said that, perhaps their unique genius was not subject to the law of averages or for that matter dictation. The EU had not put its stamp on their creation. No, not yet. Time would tell; yes, time!

To date they are having quite a difficulty with this same commodity. The engineers knew their trains and where they were going. They were convinced they could make it, as were their owners. Oh the owners, they were not only the powerhouse of these shimmering, speedy, equally noisy intrusions into our countryside; they were dictators in their own right too. No, they were not concerned about noise, laying down more tracks, all at the expense of the taxpayer and the countryside.

The latter, in this neck of the woods, a pastoral masterpiece, is threatened on all fronts - above and below. It is the lower plain we are talking about just now. High-speed tracks, these, we are led to believe, will be an immense boom to the inhabitants of this earth, the inhabitants, well at least those who have the mighty piece of plastic which secretly holds the key to their vast fortunes, or the fortunes of those who employ them. They are the business folk of this world. Somehow they too become deflated as the gusto goes out of their travelling. Their priority seats and daily newspapers, not a luxury for them, are just an essential. They seem little to ask for but are slow in achieving their objective – contentment!

The greatest schemes of mice and men are halting, grinding down, if not crumbling. They forgot, or did they, that they the owners were not the masters of all they surveyed? The humble track on which they are to run was not so well invested in. They replied, "We cannot oblige you, Mr. Train." So now it is a game of wait and see and the endless promises to the would-be users. What went wrong? Was it time, communication or sheer push? History alone will reveal.

The saga has a touch of the items called State Papers, that is information, true or false, not to be revealed now. At least not till the furor has died down and some of us with it! They will be released when it is safe to do so. Is any time ever safe for the intrigues of human nature? As I listened to the sound of the train I wondered where is speed leading all of us! All of us yes, because in some unknown way we are all its passengers.

Speed is not just on tracks, is it? It is quite amazing, if not relaxing, to sit by the Box on an ordinary day, ordinary because the world at large are not meant to be resting or taking a break. They must work or do something. That is another facet of life that enthralls me, at least when I am not caught up in it!

Like the train my mind is racing along the track and is not holding on its course. That is not an unusual phenomenon either. Oh yes I was deeply reflecting on the Box when something, not me, distracted my attention from relating my profound ideas to you! What do you see on the screen when the famous words Travel Report comes up? It is quite out of this world really, or is it? A picture of long queues on the M6 or some other highway ground to a standstill by the speed of its drivers.

Now reduced to first gear, the automatics almost non-functioning, the realm of speed has had its backlash and the rushing multitudes are left to get in touch with their powers of coping. A psychiatrist sitting on an advantage point would have a field day! The cars, well their drivers and passengers, have been dictated to. They have no way out. Silently by an unseen force they are regulated to 'a stop and sit it out session'.

The mind boggles at what must be a very high-powered adrenaline sweeping through the motor world and its kingdom. How do these humans cope or perhaps more likely retaliate? The psychiatrist examines the case before them. Quite an interesting story here, they muse. There is plenty of room here for thought!

They muse on it and not unexpectedly the thermometer of the humans reach record reaction. Speed, or loss of it, has generated deep emotions. The interesting point to note is that these human beings, encased in metal, with no control over their fate at this stage in history, have no idea of what is being depicted in the mind of the psychiatrist. Fatalism, blood pressure reaching record heights, anger, frustration and being human - even a great need of food - are all surfacing. They sit on. This is no protest, not yet, anyway! It is just ordinary speed of life or want of it.

Like the train these humans are of no account just now. They have yet a destiny to be worked out. I feel for them. You see I have experienced five hours of it and to what avail? I took advantage of a loophole and blamed my response on everyone, including traffic control, that is everyone but me! Now as I sit and see the TV. picture I wonder at my reaction. Interesting isn't it?

I ponder and quietly into my mind the words of an old song came. It must have been in my subconscious realm all the time, "Where have all the flowers gone?" they ask. Oh I go on a trot down the walk of my imagination. I ask, "Where is all the relaxation gone?" The quiet moments of sitting and letting the world go by, where are they? They were invaluable moments.

Remember listening to the chime of the old grandfather clock, which was so reluctant to hasten its steps but always willing to nap, every seven to eight days. It had a calming effect on all the family. Did you ever observe the man of the house as he, with an air of patient command, took the big key from the top of the clock and said mentally "Come on now. You have had your rest. Let me gently wind you up again."

Those days, like the flowers, seem to have disappeared long since. Yet in some strange way they are silently being sought after. They make their presence felt in the profound statement on so many brochures – "Get away from it all. Go to the sun!"

To my companions on the road with me I ask the questions, "Where is the sun? Where is the sun if it is not where you and I are?"

A GLOW OF LIGHT

- Ask yourself the question – "Where am I?"
- Time is eternal. What is the magnet that causes you to identify with this statement in your daily life?

Time

Time you are God's gift.
Where are you?
How do I see you?
Oh, You are invisible.

Is that your power,
Hidden gift of the Father?
A gift only seen
Through experience.

You are Life,
Life evoking a response.
Response is active.
Response is Love.

Teach us to treasure Life – Time.
It has many shades.
It has many twists.
Some unrecognizable to us,
But it is there.

You promised Time – Eternal.
Cause us to seek it.
Cause us to be enriched as we wait.

Waiting is power.
Waiting is stillness
Waiting is "Yes" to you.

Sell By Date

"Great Expectations", yes that was one of the top ranking films. Well I will not mention the year. It would date me! That is an interesting point. It would date me - then my sell by date would be revealed. What a thought! Story after story would possibly be laid bare. The crux though would be in the stated date, "Best before," well you know the rest.

Ah, "Best before," that includes the conditions written in small print or at times not even stated. It seems to say a lot as you purchase it, 09 - that is a long way down the road. It will be well used up by then. A sinister smile, invisible I know, appears on the face of the jar! Yes, it has its own secret and is going to keep it, at least for the present. That smile is really saying, "I will serve you under certain conditions. Have you ever read them?" A hint: they are to be found on many of the foods you purchase. So you have guessed my plot. Keep me tightly closed, let no air in and put me in cold storage in a big white chest you call the fridge. The very thought of it freezes me now! I wonder why I am to be kept in the cold?

Ah, you missed the point again. Did it not click in your mind that deep within my substance there are bugs, big and small, which can come to fruition in unsuitable conditions? Yes, they are choosy. Treat me well or I can make my presence felt.

How can this mentality of the jarred food comply with great expectations? Secondly, I ask myself, "Where and when did I imbibe these expectations?" In some way unknown to myself, I have imbibed the mass media organization aimed at potential buyers. I never realized I was such a sponge-like substance, capable of taking all into myself. How strange I feel now! I too am rendering my very being into a commodity that has a 'sell by date'!

Suddenly I am struck with a sense of unbelief, no, not great expectations. I recall the film and my first childhood memories of it: a room, dull, lifeless, windows closed and doors, for many years. The sight of those cobwebs hanging like dusty icicles from the ceiling grabs me. If this is the scene for great expectations, what scene do I present? No, I am not written off, at least for the moment. The bones are still hanging together and, in some unknown way, moving. Most times they appear to move independently of my head and the brain box within. They also, to some extent, exist in harmony with my hands and arms. So, I am happily still functioning!

I wonder what functioning is. I put down my book to have a little thought. A rest is good for the mind they say. The fire is burning but it too for some hours past depicted more life than its present smouldering flames. Flames, I muse to myself: have I got flame in my being still or is it the appropriate time to let it smoulder like the fire? Everything has its day!

A sudden jerk bolted through me. I was shot into reviewing my present thoughts; 'sell by dates', let the flame smoulder. What is great about these expectations of myself? No, not me, I thought. Better think again though. Then the whole phenomenon of the jar, its contents and the conditions it laid down if one expected great things of it, held my attention.

I remembered being a child full of expectations not fear. Joyful wishes and hopes, that is the real me. I took out my paint brushes. I am not an artist, but I figured I could sketch myself. This would not be an obvious self-portrait. What was hidden deep within me would not be publicly revealed. I was, in a way, a jar with contents.

You are right these contents were not for sale, but 'Yes, alas', or is it, 'Alas, I have a sell by date'? For the present I decided to give expression to myself in an abstract way. This, I began to feel, would be intriguing. It filled me with wonder. How would I do it? What would the finished product that is me, look like?

Suddenly I heard the words in my mind as I lost all touch with the brush and colours, "Great are your works O, Lord" or was I stopped? The great expectations changed into sudden reality. I was depicting myself, not the great artist of all time, molding my image. What were His great expectations I wondered as I put down my brush!

The night passed on and He and I seemed to spend some time sitting by my smouldering fire. Not a word was spoken. The jar of my life was being gently opened. The pressure to release the closure of my jar was gently applied. I say "gently" for I felt no pressure at all; just a Presence. I saw in it the bugs that had begun to come to life. Was it that I had not read the small or even larger print, and failed to take the conditions for my preservation to heart? I wonder why!

A GLOW OF LIGHT

- Muse on your life and the hidden small print in your story.
- Even the smouldering flame has life in it and can set the fire ablaze.
- How do you resonate with these words?

Rest with these words:

"Great are your works, O Lord."   Psalm 111

The Waters of Babylon

They were happy days down by the seaside, carefree beyond measure; a treasure we little understood. To us it was just life. You see we came from the Big City, with all its hustle and bustle. Its points of attraction were many. I can still feel the excitement within me as we neared the zoo. No, it was not as grand or commercialized as it is today, but it gripped us. What of the elephant, so large against our small stature, or the monkeys really playing to the gallery of folks at the other side of the wire! It appeared as if we were in the cage and they had full scope of self-expression and did they take it! The more 'show off' they became the more enthralled we, the children, became.

It was a powerful experience. Like the monkeys we felt free in their freedom. It was a strange feeling and even more so now as we daily get accounts of our own heritage. We blink a little as we read about our own prestigious descendancy. Then in that blink we blot out the similarity or do we? The monkeys speak their own language to us. They have a world to reveal. Who will interpret it for us, as they are more ancient than we are, perhaps more civilized if one gives them their place in the history of civilization? Gosh, I nearly wrote, salvation!

That thought provokes deeper thoughts in me. Can I, a human being, separate civilization and salvation? Are they one and not one or each part of a whole? This question poses itself before me. Both come from the one source, The Maker, Creator and Redeemer.

125

I stand and gaze at the sea. It too is taking part in this profound discussion as its waves lap in and drench the shore, before receding, Yes, the freedom of my childhood days on this same beach is somewhat interrupted today. My mind is being lured by its very existence to ponder its beginnings and never-ending ends! They, by that I mean, creation, civilization and salvation are all taking their life, their purpose and fulfillment from one source!

I stop in my train of thought. Nature itself is evoking something in me, I told myself. The years have passed and I have passed along a road too. Have I been blind to the teaching and revealing power of nature about me? It is all so much part of me and I of it. A retreat I made came to mind.

The setting was ideal: lost in the countryside amid fields of cattle grazing and the sheep nibbling away at the grass. What more could I ask for! Oh yes the walks were all part of it. Long avenues rolled down to a grade B road that invited pedestrians to safely walk its course, shaded on both sides by trees, mostly chestnut trees. The graceful, awe-inspiring poplars had their place of honour there too. All were part of this desert experience. That is what the writers call retreats. Nature was at its best in early summer. I listen and hear the poplars whisper their secret as they remind me:

"By the waters of Babylon we sat and wept,
On the poplars that grew there we hung up our harps" Psalm 137

Was I going to weep, touched by the power of a tree! Weep for what? Is that my secret, I wondered!

126

The poplars though great and tall (like the elephants) were inviting me, no, not to climb them as I did the chestnuts in my youth, but to hang up my harp. This, by the way, is the instrument I played my tunes on almost daily. Could I, would I, am I willing? The urge of nature caught me and proclaimed, " It is not so haughty a tree in spite of its erect posture in fact its loving hands are clasped in an upward movement to the heavens for me." Yes nature itself was fulfilling its creation role; it was interceding on a human's behalf.

I remembered the feeling as the tears began to rise up and swell deep within me before they made their exit through my eyes. What a feeling! It had to remain a secret all these years because no words of mine could describe it. Like the poplars it was meant to be silent. A gift of the moment, but forever!

Finally I surfaced again and began to feel normal that is dried eyed. What is wrong with tears, I thought? Nothing, just folks don't like them. They don't know what to say or, for that matter, do I! I thought again; you see it was one of those days I was capable of thinking or was it listening? A gentle wind blew. It was invigorating to my face. It will clear my head I thought and then I can proceed. Proceed with what? Well, 'Life' came the answer.

Life, like people, comes in many shapes and sizes. This I was about to experience. The words of the psalmist intruded again on my normality! This time the gentle breeze was whispering, "They hung up their harps." I have no harp, I retaliated to myself. What is all this about? But it persisted in its whisper dusting my mind – and soul for that matter. It was undeniably persistent and ruthless. I stopped again and tried to argue with the intrusion. Then the coin dropped.

I had a harp, made of many cords and strings. They were very much put together by a very young amateur. Their music, if one could call it that, was, to say the least, non-professional. It was not exactly the fault of the cords but really that of the player, that is me! I began to realize that I was the player and the music I played was very squeaky. It was enough to drive one away at times. The poplars stood still, in prayer for me, longing for me to abandon my harp and leave it on their branches. "That is impossible," I thought, "I would be lost without it. I am known by it. It is my signature tune!"

Then suddenly my world opened up. It seemed I was losing control of the terra firma that held me up. "Leave the harp on your branches." I retorted, "Never, I need it." Emotions surfaced high and deep within me – need it really? Abandon my harp, no! It was at this point that I caved in and felt my back was to the wall. There appeared to be no outlet. Not being one to give in easily, as you see, I hatched a plan of compromise: I will hang up my harp on the branches if you give me a new one. As a person I am expected to sing my song and play my harp! There was a sudden lull in the wind. The poplars stood still. In that moment I heard my harp play my tune as I never heard it before. "Have I got a new musical sense of hearing?" I asked myself. If so, that was quick. The shrill tones penetrated my ear and they were so out of tune that I, in a calm enthusiastic way, though perhaps fearful, gave my consent. My harp was hung on the whispering branch of the poplar. I stood and gazed. Suddenly I felt a great sense of relief as the words, "How can we sing on alien soil?" rose in my heart.

The years have passed, many songs have been played and sung. You know the soil was so important a factor in my reading the meter of my life with opened eyes. My squeaking, unusable harp had gone: it was replaced by a new one created out of my new soil, by the Maker Himself.

A GLOW OF LIGHT

- How does nature reveal yourself to you?
- Listen to the music within you.
- Do you need to hang up your harp?
- What instrument would you appreciate as a gift?

By the waters of Babylon. Psalm 137

The Royal Train

I walked through the front door of the sheltered housing. The entrance was homely and presented a feeling of being well cared for. The usual display of dried flowers was in a prominent position. The smell of fresh paint, the work of human hands, gave a fragrance and uplift to the fabric of the building.

My first encounter was with Jane. She looked peaceful and calm and was obviously on her way out. I knew her mother had died and inquired how she was and when was she being laid to rest. A gleam came into her eye. It, my little chat, had touched her. She seemed to say, "You are kind to remember", as she uttered her "Thank you."

At that moment Megan appeared. She always put on a brave face after her two operations, which seem to have left her quite disabled. Her hopes had not materialized. She continued to smile her way along on two sticks. Were these her real support or was it something more? I do think it was the latter. She forgot herself, and the effort she had to walk, and reached out to Joyce. The look in the latter's eyes was astonishing; she was overwhelmed. I wonder why! The thought came to me that so often people don't expect a loving reach-out from others. Perhaps the other side of the coin is they have not been recipients before! "Is this the ingredient our world needs today?" I thought to myself. What does it cost? Do we always have to wait till the sirens yell and the hazard warning lights flash? Then we wonder why it is too late.

I take my leave and head for the comfort of my own armchair and the morning cup of tea. It is time to relax. Time for myself is precious! The kettle whistles and I am enticed by its sound. That is often more easy to respond to. What good am I if I don't take care of number one first. This is a simple thought but how deep is its valley? The very thought of the valley jolted me. I would think more of this, but at another time! The words of the song "In the spring tra-la" rang in my ears. Oh yes, that is typical of me, attend to things and view the long distant road. There is a security there, no hazard immediately, and then maybe it will all pass! I mean the opportunity; then it will not stretch me. No I don't put words like these on my mind but, well, you know what I mean. They are cloaked, like all good intentions, in a most justifiable way.

I relaxed into my cup of tea. It was quite soothing to taste and even comforting. I turned on the news to see how the rest of the world was getting on. No doubt I would have my own comments on those of the newscaster. Suddenly I thought, "How does all this affect me? What does it do, no not to my thoughts but to the valley within me - seventy-five dead and -------injured? Can these be just facts?" I was meeting the real world of pain again. It was only thirty minutes since I recognized Joyce's pain and Megan's. "What is happening to me?" I asked myself. I cannot do anything about it. Helplessness is the name of the game or so I thought!

Here was a situation I had recognized, so where to from here? The casual response of fate was luring me down a road I could not, or was it would not, face? It would be an easy road to travel but where would it lead me! Momentarily I stopped. I gazed in silence at the pictures of the carnage. A numbness took possession of me. These were real people, I told myself, each with a loving family who would be distraught with grief and helplessness. I began to enter into their fate for the want of a better word. Could I feel their pain in their racked bodies? Even those who were dead had felt their own physical and mental pain as the bomb blasted them. A deep helplessness to ponder their pain took me over. The buildings I looked at were earthly and in some form or other would be replaced. They felt no pain as their massive and proudly build structures became an unseemly pile of rubble. I wondered, is there a message here for me also? Just now it is all too much for me. My earthly cup of tea loses its flavour and enticement. In fact I was oblivious of it!

Oblivious of it, yes for the present, I remember. Now I think on these moments and wonder have I been affected, not just on the surface of my rubble but deep within my valley. Can I make sense of this? No, this is not simply disaster but enduring pain. Deep, deep within me is the answer to be unearthed some day in its fullest sense.

My memory box opens up; it has its power of enlightenment and challenge. I remember my pain of loss some years past. The power of these people today has brought me in touch again with myself. I pondered all the love and understanding I received at that time. Yes it was a powerhouse of strength to me. Was that it then? I was fine to all appearances, oh yes I was. Now my dead bones within my valley speak to me again. I am beginning to relive again the utter feeling of aloneness, which this comfort and pain, mingled together, bestowed on me. Alone and yet not alone - how deep is my valley, I wondered!

I was helpless to know the depths of my own valley so how could I know that of others. My powerlessness was digging deep into me and challenging me to submit to the challenge. What was the challenge I wondered!

My mind went back to Joyce downstairs, alone with her deepest thoughts, she was Alone but not alone. She in faith, was in contact with her mother and knew the power of her presence from the upper region. She was in communication with her. Past and present seemed to come together for me. No, I was not alone. It was not a case of "Where have all the flowers gone?" Here in my presence were all the saints, the com-union of them holding our hearts afloat.

Yes I realised that Joyce's heart was afloat. Harry came along as we spoke. He was hailing the sunny morning with a large white hat I would say an extra-large hat, while his T-shirt was portraying a mighty big steam engine, in full steam, on his chest. Joyce walked over to him and pointing to the driver's cab said, "That is my husband in there." I looked at her as she spoke. He too had gone to his paradise some months before. How strange it was that a T-shirt should evoke a feeling of bonding that was so tangible in her! Love poured out from her very being in those words. "Really," I said and before I could offer another feeble word she replied, "He drove the steam train, you know, and later became the driver of the Royal Train!" How proudly those words were uttered as she thought of her dearly beloved one, now ensconced in the Royal Place of all time!

A GLOW OF LIGHT

- The valley within can be quite deep.
- Our deep feelings and treasures are very precious.
- How important is it for you to release your feelings?

    I lift up my eyes to the mountains. Psalm 121.

The Ear of Corn

I drove along the winding country roads today. It was a different experience to other days because the world of people seemed asleep in the early hour of eight-thirty a.m. Yes, it was the Day of Rest when all the hustle and bustle of getting on the road seems to take a holiday. No one commands it or invites it. It is perhaps the nature of our human being calling out 'halt!'

This morning even the road works dominated by signs of 'Diversion', 'Ramps', 'Uneven Surfaces' etc., were silent. There were no warning lights, no grinding of the big diggers, not to mention the childhood delight of burning tar. Oh how the tar told its tale if we walked on it, black sticky tar adorning our shoes as we made for home.

Home. That word conjures up many thoughts. Today I looked at the fields. There was a hint of autumn feeling about them. The dew was still on the grass and the earth was sharing its fruits, while the golden crops lay baled up in neat rows, as if asleep too. I wondered why they had the privilege of being golden. Was it because they had outlived the other fruits of the earth? That could be an assumed answer, I thought. Golden award for a service fulfilled! My mind then caught sight of another field. It was the one the Harvester of all times so often walked through, and at least on one occasion plucked the ears of corn. He had chosen it. Was that really why we call it golden?

He had given it the prestigious position of being his vehicle to carry his message. Imagine the little ear of corn has held its place in the records of time for over two thousand years! How many people have heard it mentioned? How often have I?

I felt an ache in my being. Yes I had heard it. Really! That was surprising because I suddenly realised that there are many levels of hearing even the simplest of stories. More astonishingly I then began to think that each level, each hearing has its own story. The word, my being was telling me, has an endless, timeless and many dimensions to its power. Its timeless limit beats any Guinness's Book of Records. Strange is it not, that one man plucks an ear of corn and the power of his, what appears to be a casual action, has no end! The mind boggles.

As I drove along up the hills and down into the little villages the silence of the inhabitants struck me. What was going on in their minds today, the Day of Rest? Sceptically I responded to my own question, "Not much!" Had they heard of the ear of corn or the man who plucked it? Perhaps they had. How would they rate his impact on their lives 1- 10? An intriguing question!

It was an intriguing question and it caught me off the hook. Where was I in all this? This was Rest Day. Rest Day from what, the task of daily chores and traffic jams. Maybe there is more to this question, but what? I sensed a little urge to forget it. Keep my mind on the road like a responsible citizen was surely my priority. There was no time now for daydreaming as I drove along. There was a certain amount of truth in that, alright. It is actually a wise decision.

The drive became more complicated. No, there was no traffic on the road. It was still slumber-land time. That may be the case but my mind refused to switch off. I began to get frustrated and that did not help. Then the shot of enlightenment arrowed its way through my skull, like a dart at the bull on a dartboard. The illumination of my thoughts shot like lightning. The inhabitants may be in slumber-land, but how did I know? As for the impact of the grain of wheat, how could I say what impact it had on them? I did not even speak to them not to talk of speaking to them. My spirit was beginning to sink as the truth became blatantly clear to me. I was rating them 1-10 and who am I to do so! What power or on whose authority was I doing it? The sinking feeling made me jolt. It was like a sinking ship with its treasure cargo.

I came to my senses, saw and heard myself a little more clearly. I hesitated to ask myself in this state of mind, how I would rate myself. No, this could not be put off for another time.

I went over the motorway bridge. Keep an eye out I warned myself, or you will miss the turn. Yes it will be signed. It is a clear sign, that I knew but I also knew that at this moment in time it would be quite hidden, quite secluded in the hedgerow. 'Be mindful' was the message to me 'or you will not take the right road.'

It was rather interesting, perhaps provoking or evoking, that this thought should come to me just now. BE MINDFUL. Oh, miss the sign and you may get lost or find yourself alone on another road. The journey could become hazardous I realised as there was a time factor involved. I could not afford to take the wrong road.

My thoughts seemed to be functioning at two levels now and yet synchronising. Was this strange or weird? No. There seemed to be a communication between the roadside warning and my own awareness of how I might need to rate my own response to the sleepers of the hamlet. My world was coming together. Maybe that was why I was led to take this route today. Providence I wondered, and answered, " Perhaps!" Yes there was another road but strangely enough my decision not to take it was built on solid ground. I feared I would get lost. How ironical that was. My losing myself was in fact from within!

The car kept going. Like the old horse of the eighteenth century that always knew its way home, even if the owner was a little high spirited and incapable of guiding it. The car went on very smoothly, totally unaffected in its effectiveness, by the quality if its owner. It was well It did, as I needed to get there.

Where was I going? Oh, I forgot to tell you. This was no ordinary journey. I was going to kneel at the feet of the man that plucked the ear of corn. I had the best motivation. It was Sunday and like all good followers I would give him his time, even if it was rationed. Today was special. We, that is I and my friends, would thank him for the long and faithful life of a friend. In fact we would celebrate around the Master. It would be a moment of moments when, like all invited guests, we would feast of the food at the Master's table.

It was ironic that I took the road I did. The road and the fields, one could not separate them - even with hedges, spoke to me. The message was loud and clear and it profoundly touched me. I hope I responded as I was, in some little way, plucked out of my cosy ego. The impact of His word on my mind is timeless and never ending. Once heard, it can never go away. He did say "I am with you always", didn't He?

I took the right turn and got there on time. Time waits for no man (or woman) or so they say. I feel time waited for me that day. No, not the ticking of the clock, but He who made time!

I met up with the others, all were in good form and happy to celebrate the birthday. As I knelt, I too was happy and rejoiced for myself. The desire to sing a new song was deep within me – a song of roads and fields. It was a song that revealed the Master plucking the ear of corn in my heart. To me it was truly a golden, priceless ear that he presented to me. One that more than any other gift, I would hopefully treasure. His way of taking me along to His banquet with oil in my lamp was silently my secret within me.

Inevitably like all folks we did celebrate. Before we were blessed to go our separate ways, the cake, need I say more, blazed its way in on its grandstand. It was a real celebration and like my mind on the road, it functioned on two levels.

A GLOW OF LIGHT

- Be still; listen to the murmurings within you.
- What ear of corn needs to be plucked out in your field?

Scripture reference: John 8, 8

If there is anyone among you who has not sinned let him cast the first stone.

The Message Received

The telephone rang and the voice at the other end made itself known to me. I had met him though I could not say I knew him for that word has many connotations. With the passing of time, like many other words in our daily vocabulary, it too changes its meaning according to the "in" group that verbalises it.

The power of the "in" group is strange isn't it? Expectations, or what they call expectations, are unrolled before us in today's world. Was it always the same? Maybe, though life must have been more stable in the past. The good old days, good for whom I thought! Yes I was on the phone, even it has its advantages, and disadvantages.

You see I had just returned home and had thought of putting my feet up for a few moments and letting the world go by. Then I realised there may be a phone message for me. I don't know who I expected to phone me at this hour anyway. Sure enough the mystery voice, which never seems to change, greeted my ears. "You have one new message etc." With an inquiring mind I press the button. At that point the caller made himself known to me. It was a change from all those anonymous people who want to sell you something, usually the greatest product, or even policy, you never heard of. A life insurance policy – how does that grip you? All promises for earth but none for hereafter, I thought. What an investment that would be! Great, depending on which way you looked at it. This insurance through the small print, so small to insure you can't read it, does not declare its real pack of cards. That would give the secret away for good if anyone spread the word around. It could be Doom's Day for the policy promoters.

The voice went on. A lady near you has been burgled. How did he know? He explained that to me. I had begun to think he had telescopic mind power as he lived miles from this side of the big city. I listened to him. Yes the lady had been burgled and she was very upset. Naturally so, I reflected. But how did he know I asked?

Life can be strange in its actions. He told me two men had come to do a job in his house and they told him, because they had been called upon to repair the damage done to her house. How thoughtful of them to seek help! I began to comprehend the power of the word. It was like pigeon carrier. My mind began its fantasy trip and I could see the three of them on this wonderful day talking about her and deciding to phone me. I say wonderful because, to the world in our neck of the woods, it was making history. We were having a heat wave! I just love the sun. Somehow or another it melts me so I willingly drift away from work.

Away from the world called work. My thoughts lapse again. I wonder is there any insurance against it! Perhaps surfacing the World Wide Web might surprise me with one. Having said that nothing about it surprises me any longer, not even the strong impact it seems to have on me as it seems to stand still and say, "No more work today" or is the term 'crashed'? I will not describe my inner thoughts when that happens.

The Lady, to get back to her and the caller, her phone number was ----. I took it down and he repeated it. Then the crunch came, "Could I visit her?" he asked. Wow, I put down the phone. By the way he wasn't sure he had the right name! That is helpful I thought! Many usual thoughts went floating through my mind.

It was Monday morning. I had tried to set the day aside. I knew what had to be done and time was limited and now it was fast rolling on. Was my day about to be changed forever by this call? Yes, it was a call I felt compelled to respond to, in a sense respond to the unknown. "Man proposes and God disposes," I thought. "That is a fatalistic response," I muttered to myself and then wondered where I was in this scene. Insurance policy I reflected or is it!

Then I lifted the phone. It rang and rang. She wasn't there or perhaps was too afraid to answer. Am I making things worse for her I wondered. Then I realised that if she did answer I may not have the right name, just one that sounded like it perhaps. Relieved at not getting a reply I put the phone down again.

Then I made one last attempt to contact her, and I say last. There is a lady in the village who knows everybody, or so I thought. I phoned her. No, she didn't know her. Then the jewel words were spoken, "Have you looked in the directory? See if there is a name that matches the sound plus the number you dialled." How amazing! The most direct way or so it appeared at that moment, had escaped my cognitive process. I thanked her. "Well," she said, "that's the result of my police training!"

Investigation, that's what they call it. It has reminiscence of a James Bond film. I took a deep sigh as I replaced my phone. Investigate, I pondered. That is going to consume my time and energy as I go through the new directory received this week. Yes, it is up to date but I am still no further on.

I began to think of the little old lady. Was she alone, had she any family, were the police taking care of her? Somehow the more I thought the more I saw my task disappear! This was a strange reaction. Oh, I felt sorry for her. It should never have happened but where was I in all of this? Time would tell but one thing I now knew was that I had to make contact. I had to investigate the book of words and numbers. How revealing that would be!

I sat down before launching on my new course for the day. My previous best plan for the day had not safeguarded my freedom or had it?

Life is full of surprises and where it takes you is the greatest of all, I thought. A calm came over me. Were all my little plans for today so important that life would cease if interrupted for another day? I looked out the window and saw that the sunshine was calling me on a different path. There are a lot of different flowers in the garden of my life also and this lady was the one today. Carefully she must be attended to. How, still remained a mystery but it had to be investigated. It may be a job for Doctor Who but the mystery would be revealed.

Calmness prevailed. The impossible tracking down became possible. All I had to do was to move slowly like the snail as the leaves of the pages unearthed the mystery in words.

Oh, the mystery of words, spoken and unspoken cannot be silenced, I thought!

A GLOW OF LIGHT

- Consider this phone message came to you. How would you be likely to respond?
- How have you been challenged by this story?

The Music of the Word

Your Word Lord
Is music to my ears;
The ears of my mind,
The ears of my heart.

What sound can be more awakening,
More penetrating?
It fills my soul with stillness.
It emanates with power.

Wonderful the silence of your word, Lord
What thought of man could compose it?
Yours is an inward, outward moving song.

Its rhythm is clear.
It sparkles like diamonds on the shore of life.
It is precious to behold.
It is recognisable to the listener.

Create in us O Lord
A dwelling place for your word
A place that recognises its privilege.
For who can fathom, touch or speak that word?
You alone give it power.

Power recreates,
Power illuminates,
Power brings to birth the secrets of your love.

Helpless

The room seemed to stand still in its very fabric. An air of non-communication with the world outside it, prevailed; that was till the train passed by. It was a humble train of just three carriages but it had its own purpose to fulfil.

I wondered what life would be like without a train? In times past their lines were closed down. They were considered obsolete. Now with the advance of engineering the humble train is once again sought. We are told it is the way to travel. That is a point, if only the trains really ran on time and in areas where there is little or no transport. Pressure groups add their weight to this argument as the powers that be placate us with targets and standards. Well are these words really only a smoke screen for non-action!

Smoke screens are in reality very invisible commodities to the naked eye, but to the inner eye of the observer they are patiently clear; so clear one can truthfully say there is nothing behind them - no thought, no message and certainly no action exists. They are just one more platitude that flow from the human mouth and pen in hand! Oh, there is no need for one to get excited. Rather adopt the mentality of "it will never happen" and get on with your life.

That's an interesting outlook. Get on with your life; pull the shutters of your train down and steam along your own line. What a wonderful time you would have or would you? Isolation, isolation is what they call it.

I had a funny thought. Imagine the whole human race, each individual of the billions, each going their own way. Oh yes, with the shutters down too! What a world of lines; electrified and even petrified, running horizontally and perpendicularly on the surface of the world. Their main keynote being, "Keep your shutters down and move". There would be billions of lines with no network, many ending in dead ends! I wonder is there any truth in image at all. The mind boggles. Is it all too farfetched, mad to say the least of it?

It's only an analogy, but it is the human race that is involved. Involved, that is an interesting point, involved yet not being involved in anything outside their own personal orbit. Really! Are there some people like that? What planet do they inhabit? More important how did they get there? How did they find their own railway line? A railway line with no expectation of commuters! Can you imagine it? What a relief it would be, if only once in a while the rush of life vanished and the platforms were more hospitable to the passengers; affording room to stand or even walk along without the familiar obstacles they call baggage!

Well my thoughts go back to the folks on their own rail link. A link to where I ask myself. Surely one cannot link up with oneself or can they? This is a point worth thinking about in a leisurely moment.

True I told myself as my mind posed yet another question. How did they get on this line anyway? Their train with its shutters down must be quite a lonely place to be. Isolation can be like a bug that slowly winds its way. Oh, just like the one line train with no connection point I thought. Strange isn't it, but the thought began to fascinate me. I would not mind that for a day or two I thought! But even then, knowing me, I would be more than tempted to lift the shutters and out of curiosity see how the rest of the world was behaving. Curiosity, well, not just that I must admit. You see I am one of those many people who need others to travel along with.

My co-travellers all have their own place, we diverge, go on our own link-lines only to converge again at some other station. Then the story of our world begins again to unravel itself as we delight in sharing and recalling our happenings. Something happens in those moments. Little insights flash, fears and joys get their rightful place. The friendship blossoms into a deeper understanding of what it is that keeps the world around us.

Ticking over, well, you know what I mean. Your "get up and go" has been serviced and the wide horizons of your planet's landscape calls you on! Your down note is replaced by vibrant energy and the will to travel on for another day. Happy travelling!

That wish evokes something in me. I lapse back to the thought of the lone traveller on their own non-connecting line. I try to enter their world. What has brought them to this point? How sad I feel for them and one will never know how sad or otherwise they are. Why? Because the shutters are down and the message they give to the passer-by is, "Keep out. Private domain." This is the power, I thought, that empowers their one line train to run. Run it may do, but function? I leave that to you to decide.

Have you ever been there or watched others from a distance? I have watched them. Helpless is what one calls the response it creates in you. You find yourself parked at the gate of no return and weep inwardly for a joyful life crushed by an unseen force. I think of a person I know. They are so real a person to me but to themselves life is not real. Hope does not seem to spring at all, even for a moment. They can't make sense of their lives and fear to utter the words. Their hearts call out silently and they don't know what for. It's a lonely world, this one line track.

As I stop and think I feel helpless. This not an easy feeling to bear but it is alright. It is not an unusual reaction. Suddenly my thoughts are jerked by the words "Behold your mother" and her presence becomes a tower of strength in my helplessness.

A GLOW OF LIGHT

- What kind of commuter on life's journey are you?
- Do you dare to raise the shutters forever?
- Stand with your Mother at the foot of our Lover's Cross.

Mary

You are a woman
Beloved by Him who created you.
You shine like the sun
Amid the gloom of the world's pain.

Herald of joy
You are filled with hope.
Saddened, not crushed
By the world you behold.

Come then from the mountain's stream
Echo the Godhead's praise fulfilled.
We are your children,
Loved upon earth, heavenward bound.

Fill us with your hope.
Cause it to leap in us.
Cause us to leap with it,
Carrying your people
Along the green, often spoiled
Fields of life.

Up and Away

The sun is high in the sky today. It was to have been one of those remarkable days for a group of people, for two men in particular. Their expectations were high and published. It was to have occurred yesterday but the weather, they were assured, would be more suitable to their achievements today!

Achievements yes, a wonderful fact really! They were to go up in a balloon and break the height record of 21 to 25. There was no problem. All was in order. Higher than Concord they would go. Interesting as even Concord has been grounded by factors outside its own control. I mean the plane's control, no not that of their owners and builders. It had been hailed as a marvellous feat. Like many of its predecessors in the world of achievements it has met its doomsday. Oh yes, there are one or two folks ready to invest in it still; this is not for the glory of the plane but to increase their own inestimable wealth. That seems at this moment in time to have an endless life span or does it?

Their pictures came up on the screen and they are, or so the reporters say, deflated. Are they and on what authority is this statement made I wonder? They appear, well it would be stretching it too far to say they are smiling, but they don't appear dejected. No, not by a long shot! You remember the balloon had a hole in its indestructible fabric and the helium escaped. The wonders of the modern world are unique but not full of power. They depend on many other components to stay alive in the world of achievements. The helium needed the balloon and the balloon needed the helium and both surprisingly enough needed the gentle touch of the weather, summer weather with its favourable clouds.

Today the weather prevailed but the human touch of the mighty engineered balloon was found wanting. I was driving along the road and wondered how they really felt today. Are they even going to give us the true story or keep to the given line? Theirs was really a response in hope – "Hope springs eternal." They said they would seek the fault and try again next year. They are men of courage, well yes, but they said it would be just another day of playing with a balloon!

Playing with a balloon! That sounds like a child's statement but then we are all children at heart. Didn't He once say, "Unless you become as little children". There was a note of warning there, silently spoken. It also contained a hint at the end result. Strange, the result would be a mighty achievement, fantastic really! Well yes, this achievement I seem to remember does not depend on the weather or any remarkable engineering work. This stunned me. I drove along thinking how my car, with its ticking engine and four wheels, was kept together!

I was led on, hopefully or wishfully thinking, hoping that all the bolts and screws were in place and fastened tightly. I once had that feeling before when we reached the heights of the sky and thought of the sheer drop. The voice of one of the hostesses rang in my ears. Ladies were asked to take off their shoes before making for the exit with their life jackets on. The very thought made me feel so frozen, I could have come straight out of the freezer; feelings wise I mean!

Then it suddenly occurred to me that life is one big risk made up of a lot of helium. The latter inflates us and in spite of or because of what is presented to us in a package, we float on. One stage leads to another and then the warning bells ring out "Don't look back unless the view is good."

Those two men they were going to have a field day in more sense than one. From high above, like the birds, they would view the world below them – habitations and inhabitants. Then what would follow? That is the stickler; where to from here? My mind tells me "Don't call my bluff. You know the endless opportunities and risks, and shall I mention the word achievements, that await them. Like an endless saga, what would the end be?

Memories rolled back for me. So much imagination powered my life and so much was not achieved. Did it matter? At the time yes, but today? No. I am learning what to be a child in the real sense means. I thought of a number of older people I knew in life. Their presence seemed to ring out a note of "I have lived, experienced it all, and the end though not in sight, they are mindful of it. The great achievement of a lifetime would be theirs. The old man and his wife, sitting in the garden, as I rushed by at forty miles an hour, were living that moment to the full. They talked of the flowers, perhaps even of their younger days. They just sat and were present to each other. The bliss of love I thought! What is love? Can we humans define it? The long scroll of their unknown achievements was indelibly written on their unknown gold medal!

I paused to think that night and the couple spoke to me of a child. They sit and run about in joy completely caught up in the present moment. How they get lost in weaving daisy chains. It is wonderland for them. They have their feet on the ground and no other land exists for them. Oh to be a child!

I pondered as I put my paper down. Maybe this is the enterprise I have to embark on. The touch of the engineer will have to be from above and within and the achievement a surprise and I remember the words "No eye has seen or ear heard what wonders the Lord has prepared for those who love Him."

A GLOW OF LIGHT

- What significance has this story for your life?
- With what effect does this achievement story penetrate your being?

Scripture Reference: Matt 18: 3

Sit quietly and ponder the words "Unless you become as little children you shall not enter the kingdom of heaven."

EPILOGUE

Being

Where is there a God so great as our God?
He has reached the depths of my being,
Sought it out
And sought a response from me
Deep in the shelter within me where He lies.

Hidden and yet invisible,
Silent yet pulsating,
Leading yet observing,
Calm but powerful,
Immense in His majesty.

Who can find Him
Except in the depths of their being?
Balm is the love
He pours on our wounds
Softly His touch
Bringing forth life,
Life without end.

Who is like our God?
None is like our God.
You search for him in vain
If you wander away
From the depths of your being.

So noble and precious a place
Your being,
Home for your God.
There is no way in
Except through your being.

Life itself emanates from within.

Gather around your being.
Sit silently with it
Allow the pulse from within
To stir your very existence.

17373845R00091

Printed in Poland
by Amazon Fulfillment
Poland Sp. z o.o., Wrocław